doorways to discipleship

Collected and compiled by
Winkie Pratney

Design and Artwork by
Paul Annan

Communication Foundation Publishers
P. O. Box 386
Lindale, Texas 75771

Doorways to Discipleship
Copyright 1975   Winkie Pratney
Printed in the United States of America

Table of Contents

MENTAL

PHYSICAL

PREFACE

You are young in God — but you belong to Him.

This is a book for the young: The young in spirit, the young in faith, the young in living for Jesus. It is not a hard book, or a complicated one; but I think you will find it a helpful one. For one thing, it will show you how to do some of the things you know you ought to do as a new Christian — and for another, it will show you how to do them well.

This book is called *Doorways To Discipleship* because it is like a house, the house of YOUR life. Each chapter is like a doorway to an entire area of your life — and each room of this house must be given wholly over to Christ as His rightful property.

When you became a child of God, everything you had and were was transferred back to Jesus, who rightfully owned you in the first place. His you were, and when you lived for yourself and did not care about Him, you were really stealing yourself from Him. Then you gave up and gave in to His love — and He accepted you back. Now it is His task to go over your home, room by room, and point out doors that have never been opened to His examination.

Each door of this house is a doorway of dedication. It is also a doorway of discovery, because no one really can be a Christian unless they give all that they have and are back to God to begin with. That means that when you get saved, you give everything you have to Christ that you know about. In this book, we will look at some areas that you might not have thought about when you first found new life in Jesus, but that nevertheless belong to Him.

Do not think in terms of surrendering these areas to Him. They are His already, by right and by ownership. Think instead of finding new areas of your life so that you can serve Him more fully; think instead of discovering deeper and deeper levels of loving living that can be used by the Master. Think of each section of this book as a reminder of what is His and how it can be better used for His service.

Take each doorway, and each "room" carefully, one at a time. If you like, first of all take the test that is printed in the back of this book — the "house blueprint." (refer to page 229) Go through it and at each "room" ask yourself carefully: "Has there ever been a time when I have consciously and intelligently given this area of my life over to His use? Has He taught me how to use this 'room' for His glory? Do I serve Him in this area of my life?" If you are not sure, or if the answer is a "No," then leave that square blank. For all others, color in the squares of the chart. When you are finished you will have a blueprint of your life in its usefulness for God. This will also show you what you need to work on right away.

Now, use the sections of the book to show you how to bring the areas you need help in under His direction and discipline. True discipleship is conforming your life to as much of Christ and His wisdom as you know of Him today. To be a true disciple of Jesus is to live a life of constant growth, change, and challenge as Jesus molds you step by step into the kind of man or woman you should be.

So read on — and more. DO what you need to do. It is not to the hearers of His Word that He speaks and touches, but to those who DO His will. This is your task, and your great privilege. And as you walk through these rooms of your house that is His temple, you will discover wonderful things within each doorway—your doorways to discipleship.

Winkie Pratney

I

THE BASEMENT: Motives

Here we are. We are starting right at the bottom of your house. It's dark down here! No one usually comes to the basement except to clean it up or to look for something hidden. We have come down to check the foundations of your house. There may be a lot down here to clean if Jesus is going to stay here. Let's turn on the light, open the door — and go down the stairs!

The Lord Jesus introduced something radically new into the principles that govern people. Old forms and rules that had meant so much in the past were to be made better; motives and impulses were to be all-important. By the thoughts of his heart, man was to be judged by God; LOVE was to be the foundation, the "golden rule."

But what makes something "right" or "wrong"? How can you tell if it is or isn't?

Ecclesiastes 3:11 says, "HE (God) has made EVERY-THING beautiful in His time." Funny, but almost all "wrong" things are "right things" MISUSED. Take *food*: It's good to eat, but excess is gluttony, a SIN in God's eyes. *Sex*, in its right place, is God-given, beautiful, and fun—but misused it is a terrible sin. It's not so much WHAT you do, but WHY you do it that really counts. This is the basement of every house. It is the sort of foundation everything we do is built on. What is the foundation of YOUR life? What "base" have you built on?

Now, people can only be led in two ways: by *force* or by *trust*. We can live either by RULES (based on hope or fear) or by LOVE — trust for the one who leads us. Trust and love is *God's* way. It is His foundation for the family; the wellspring of romance and marriage; the Biblical basis for harmony in a town, city or nation. When love goes, bribery and punishment are all that is left to keep things in line. And this, the rule of hope and fear, is the way of the world.

Now he who is not a true Christian is selfish at heart. He still lives by threats or bargains. He acts to collect bribes or avoid punishment. Before he chooses, he wants to know if there is something in it for him. And only warning and threats stop him from messing up others' happiness.

So our world has only two kinds of people. The difference between these two is radical. They may do similar things outwardly. They may agree on many things, even live in the same home, go to the same school or church, do the same jobs, play the same games. But their "basements" are different. One life is founded *God's* way. The other is built on sand. Think of two children in a home: One obeys his Dad because he trusts him. He has a faith in his father that works by love. The other is self-centered. He wants all that he can get from his father, so he does what he *has* to do. He obeys only under force when he doesn't like it, because he doesn't really care about his Dad's happiness. So are the lives of the true Christian and the false. God's true child has confidence and trust in Jesus that leads him to wholly give himself to God's will. The phony, like the devil, has only a partial submission and a selfish heart. He "believes and trembles." (James 2:19) He wants to be saved for his own safety, but he never gives in at heart to be led and ruled by the Lord. This is the religion of law. It is wholly unlike Jesus. It is outward only; artificial and plastic. And when God starts on us, He starts with our hearts.

How is YOUR heart? What is your "basement" like? Does Jesus *really* live in your innermost man? Have you made that unreserved surrender; that trust that leads to peace of mind and joy of soul; that whole-hearted giving of yourself to Christ? This book can do no greater task than urge you to do this. *Doorways To Discipleship* will mean very little to one who has never become a disciple. Here is where you begin: Stop reading this section if you are not wholly God's — get on your knees and do the FIRST THING — give God your heart! If you need help, go to the section "How To Be Saved" at the back of this book.

HOW TO TELL IF SOMETHING IS WRONG

God has put a warning light in your soul. Have you ever seen an "idiot light" in a car? It is a little red or amber light that comes on when your oil or water is low. (It tells you when it glows that you are an idiot if you go on!) Your basement "idiot light" is your CONSCIENCE. Your conscience is not just an idea that your parents gave you. It is a gift from God. It works well when treated right. Listen to it and you will save yourself much pain and heartache. Sometimes it can be badly misused or fed wrong ideas.

It works like a watch. It is supposed to be set by comparing it to the standard time, the right time according to standards set strictly by the laws of the universe. But if you fool with it or knock it around, it, just like a watch, will either not work *at all* or tell you the *wrong* time. Don't mess with your conscience. Check it out against the standard of God's Word regularly. And when it tells you the truth, *listen*. Don't bash it just to see if it will tell you something else you'd rather do instead. After a while, with rough treatment, it will. But you will be sorry. Conscience gives warnings that are dangerous and destructive to ignore.

Sometimes it is hard to know whether a thing is right or wrong. Now, obvious things like murder or rape, robbery or outright lies are easy to tab. But there are some situations when it is hard to know. Here is a little test to help you in such cases. There is only one condition. You must be BRUTALLY honest. We can get to like something that is wrong so much that we will ignore, shrug off, or forget what God says about it. But SIN is SIN. We must answer to God one day for our lives, if we don't listen to His instruction now.

Before you start, ask the *Holy Spirit* to use these questions to search your heart. The Bible says something about our hearts that we do well to remember when we are trying to decide if something is wrong or not. It says, "The heart of man is deceitful above all things and desperately wicked — who can know it?" The answer to that question is the Holy Spirit. He knows us; He knows our hearts. We don't always even know WHY we do some things because of hidden motivations behind what we said or did. But He does. And He will show us if it will help us become finer, stronger men and women.

If your motives are being tested, you may be tempted to "rush" through this test. Don't. Take your time. The results are at the end of this section of the book. Don't look until you have gone right through the questions. Do the test as if you were doing it for someone else. In each question there are two alternatives. One is why you are doing something; the other is why you are not. Use whichever form of question that applies in your case. Read CAREFULLY. Got a pencil to check things? Alright — here goes.

TEST FOR WRONG MOTIVES

(1) Does your action *puff you up* in the eyes of others? Will it make you feel a little more superior or informed or experienced than them? Are you "dropping names"? OR — do you think you CAN'T do it because you are shy? Pretty useless? Worthless? Not one who is "worthy" of doing it? Are you saying to yourself, "God could never use me anyway"? Maybe NOT doing it will injure (a) your social standing, (b) position, (c) reputation among the men and women of the secular and ungodly world?

(2) Is your action basically for your *OWN GAIN*? Be honest. Is the reason WHY you are offering or thinking of doing this to bring YOU the supreme pleasure in the situation? Will the alternative demand some sort of sacrifice or self-denial on your part?

(3) Does your action feed a *HABIT* of body or mind? Is it a look, touch, sound, or thought that can form a controlling slavery? Are you doing your own thing, or is your own thing doing you? OR: Will making this choice require a radical BREAK with something you have been doing that you suspect is harmful, or someone you have been selfishly attached to for a long time? Everytime you think of that person or thing, do you feel an uncontrollable urge?

(4) Do you *resent or dislike* a person/persons involved? Are you doing what you are doing because this is one way you can (a) "show" them; (b) get back at them; or (c) get even for the past? OR: Are you NOT doing it because (a) they don't deserve it, (b) they never helped you, so why should you help them? (c) they hurt you, and have never apologized?

(5) Are you acting because you are *AFRAID* of what the "in-crowd" will say? Afraid of being "left out" or on the

shelf? OR: Are you leaving something undone because you might be laughed at or criticized for doing it, even though you know it is right?

(6) Are you *ENVIOUS* of the other person/persons involved? Does it make you mad to see them get something you don't have or couldn't get? Do you feel "put out" if they find out or get hold of something you thought was exclusively yours? OR: Are you doing what you are doing to "keep up," because everyone else does it too?

Take your test. Then turn to the end to find the "hidden reason" behind your actions or thoughts. Don't cheat now! DO THE TEST FIRST! Then look.

LOVE — *God's* love — is the only life-style that can give us the right motives. When our WHOLE DESIRE is to please Him, no matter how imperfect our work, He can smile on it. He can put up with anything except selfishness. God is like a loving Father who looks on our work for Him as a Dad looks with affection on his child's first homemade present. It may look a little shapeless, rough, or grubby. But He sees the love that was put into it, and it is worth far more to Him than it looks. Now, to love God simply means to UNSELFISHLY PUT HIM FIRST in everything we do. It is to choose His highest good and to live this way with all others. It is more than attraction, more than friendship. It is the result of a life surrendered to the God Who is all that real love is. And it is the mark of every Christian.

"TEENETHICS" —
MORE HELP FOR MAKING CHOICES

Here are some extra points to help you decide what is best. All of these are useful only to underline and support a direction from the Holy Spirit and the Word of God.

(1) *What would JESUS do?* (This must deal with the PRINCIPLE and not just the actual situation. It is true that it is hard to imagine Jesus with a cigarette in His mouth, but it is also hard to imagine Him driving a car.) But think:

Would Jesus take part in this kind of activity? "For even to this were you called, because Christ also suffered for us, leaving us an *example* that you should follow in His steps." (I Peter 2:21) "He that says He abides in Him, ought himself to walk *even as He walked*." (I John 2:6)

(2) *Is it TRUE? KIND? NECESSARY?* Ask yourself these three questions when you are tempted to pass on something you heard about someone else. "He that has knowledge spares his words." (Proverbs 17:27a) "But let your communication be 'Yes, Yes' or 'No, No' — for whatever is more than these is of evil." (Matthew 5:37) "Pleas-ant words are as honeycomb, sweet to the soul and health to the bones." (Proverbs 16:24) "Let your speech be always with grace, seasoned with salt that you may know how to answer every man." (Colossians 4:6) "Speaking the truth in love . . ." (Ephesians 4:15)

(3) *Is it EXPEDIENT?* (Is it useful, the best thing to do under the circumstances? Does it best fit the facts and truth you have?) Does it *EDIFY?* (Improve you morally.) Can it form a *HABIT?* (A power that can develop so deep a hold on your life that it actually begins to control you.) "All things are lawful for me, but I will not be brought under the power of any." (I Corinthians 6:12b) "All things are lawful for me, but all things edify not." (I Corinthians 10:23b)

(4) *Is it a WING or a WEIGHT?* (Will it help your Christian life or hinder it?) *Wings* are God's BEST; they are the finest, most useful things you can do with the time He has given you. God says, "Redeeming the time, because the days are evil . . ." (Colossians 4:5) "Covet earnestly the best gifts." (I Corinthians 12:31) *Weights* are anything that will slow you down. They don't have to be *bad;* they can be *good* things that are not the *best.* "Wherefore seeing we are

compassed about by so great a cloud of witnesses, let us lay aside every weight, and the sin which does so easily beset us, and let us run with patience the race that is set before us, looking to Jesus . . ." (Hebrews 12:1-2a)

(5) *Does it HONOR THE LORD?* Will it bring greater glory to His Name? Will He be pleased about it? Will people think more about Him and His love if they know about this? "He that has My commandments and keeps them, he it is that loves Me; and he that loves Me shall be loved of My Father, and I will love him and show Myself to him." (John 14:21) "Them that honor Me, I will honor." (I Samuel 2:30)

(6) Will it make a weaker Christian *STUMBLE?* Will someone be hindered in the Christian life by seeing what you do, even if your motives are right in it? Will your action be misunderstood by others who look up to you as an example? "But take heed lest by any means this liberty of yours becomes a stumbling block to them that are weak . . . through your knowledge, shall your weak brother perish, for whom Christ died? But when you sin against the bretheren, and wound their weak conscience, you sin against Christ; wherefore, if meat makes my brother offended, I will eat no meat while the world stands, lest I make my brother offended." (I Corinthians 8:9-13)

(7) *Can I PRAY about it?* With an UNTROUBLED MIND? Can you commit it wholly into the Lord's hands? Do you feel His peace in your heart about doing it? "And whatsoever you do, do it heartily as to the Lord, and not to men; for you serve the Lord Christ; but he that does wrong shall receive for the wrong which he has done; and there is no respect of persons." (Colossians 3:23-25) "Be anxious for nothing; but in everything, by prayer and supplication with thanksgiving, let your requests be made known to God; and the peace of God, which passes all understanding, shall keep your hearts and minds through Christ Jesus." (Philippians 4:6-7)

(8) *Can you PRAISE GOD for it?* Get on your knees and THANK HIM for it? If NOT: It's better to leave it alone. Learn the parable of the shirt collar. A man asked his wife,

"Dear, is this shirt collar dirty or not?" She called back, "If it's *doubtful*, it's *dirty*." The Bible says, "Whatsoever is not of faith, is sin." Charles Fin-ney said, "Do not say in your prayers, 'Oh Lord, if I have sinned in this thing, or Lord, forgive me the sin.' If you have done anything of which you doubted the lawfulness, you *have* sinned, whether the thing itself be right or wrong. And you must repent and ask forgiveness." Do not com-promise with doubtful deci-

sions. God will honor any sacrifices made for Him. "Let heavenly thoughts fill your mind; don't waste time worry-ing about earthly problems. You should not let the desires of this world phase you. Most of all, let LOVE be your guide . . . and in all speech and actions, let them be as an example of Jesus Christ the Lord, giving thanks to God and the Father by them." (Colossians 3:2, 3, 14, 17)

TEST RESULTS

(1) *PRIDE* — Your actions draw too much attention to yourself. Love is not puffed up with its own importance; love neither puffs up or puts down, exalts or depresses you.

(2) *SELF* — Your action is self-centered. "Though I give all my goods to feed the poor, give my body to be burned, and have not love, I am nothing. Love "seeks not her own."

(3) *LUST* — You are falling victim to an enslaving habit. Love is not easily provoked, does not behave itself unbe-comingly. Love knows both discipline and self-control.

(4) *HATE* — Love knows how to bear pressure; it is kind. It hardly even notices when others do it wrong. It does not hold grudges; it always expects the best of people.

(5) *FEAR* — Perfect love "casts out fear," including the fear of the crowd or of criticism. Love "does not rejoice in iniquity, but rejoices in the truth, or love "bears all things."

(6) *ENVY* — Love does not covet, and is not marked by the grasping spirit of the world. Love is satisfied with what it has; it knows how to "be abased and abound"; it knows how to live with plenty or live in loss. Love is not envious or jealous of other's good things.

If you get a positive answer on any of the questions asked in the wrong motive guide, your action is wrong and under the displeasure of God. These are the "opposite" fruits of love as God has defined it in I Corinthians 13 and in other passages of Scripture.

SCRIPTURES FOR STUDY

Verses for heart-searching: Matthew 7:17-18; Mark 12:30-31; II Corinthians 5:14-15.

ALL THINGS good to God: Genesis 1:31; Romans 14:14; Titus 1:15.

God looks on the HEART: I Samuel 16:7; John 7:24; II Corinthians 5:12.

SHALL I or NOT? I Corinthians 6:12; 10:23; Hebrews 12:1-2a; I John 2:15; Colossians 3:17; James 4:1.

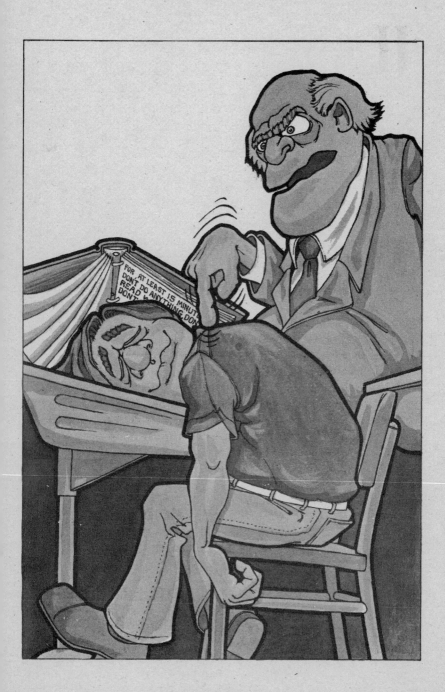

II

THE GALLERY: Meditation

It can be a beautiful room, the picture gallery. Here, along the walls, are scenes that can bring back many lovely memories. The gallery is a place in your soul which you can go to when you need a quiet time to think. Here, in the house of *your* life, it is the room of a daily time to "chew over" problems and goals. Jesus wants access to your picture gallery — and He wants to help you hang the pictures.

WHO AM I?

SYMPTOMS OF GROWING UP — It happens to us all. Here are the things you will go through:

(1) *INSECURITY:* You're pulled in two directions. You don't want to be a kid, but you're scared to be an adult. You aren't sure of yourself at all. You get shy; sometimes you're afraid to ward off inferiority feelings, and sometimes you disguise them with a superior manner that makes you a pain in the neck. But — it always happens. You need time to get on your feet, to find out who you are. And until then,

you'll have a few painful falls and get hurt where it really hurts — inside. But cheer up! God knows who you are.

(2) *RESTLESSNESS:* You can't seem to settle down. You're impatient with yourself or others; sometimes you don't even know why! You don't quite know where you're going or what you want when you get there, but one thing is sure, you're on your way!

(3) *INCONSISTENCY:* You're up one day, down the next. Your emotions whirl like a merry-go-round. Your voice won't behave itself. You make great resolutions today and break them all tomorrow. You are close friends with someone this day, complete strangers the next; laughter one minute, and the next, tears. If anyone tries to help keep you on the track, you even get a little resentful. You think it should be easy for your friends and parents to understand. But IS IT? And DO THEY?

(4) *INDECISION:* A lot of times you simply can't make up your mind about anything. "Should I or should I not go there?" "Should I ask her to go out with me?" "Shall I wear this old comfortable thing or this new, untried one?" "Should I hide from my friend what my home and parents are like, or let it all hang out?" But no adult can tell YOU what to do!

SEVEN BASIC NEEDS

People who study the youth culture say we need *seven basic things* to keep us happy. Here they are. See what belonging to God does for you in each of them. In a world where it is hard to find out who you are, or why you are here, He is the One Person you can always rely on Who will never leave you nor forsake you.

(1) *SECURITY:* We need to know that we will be cared for. God has promised to do just that if our lives are in His hands: "And I give to them ETERNAL LIFE; and they shall never perish, neither shall any man pluck them out of my hands." (John 10:28)

(2) *A SENSE OF BELONGING:* We need to feel we belong to the right crowd. There are a lot of crowds you can give your loyalty to. Only one is eternally worth belonging to. That's God's team. When we know the Lord, we are all part of His great family. What a privilege to be called by the King of all Kings! Jesus said, "I pray for them; I pray not for the world, but for them which You have given me; for they are Yours. And all Mine are Yours, and Yours are Mine; and I am glorified in them." (John 17:9-10)

(3) *KNOWLEDGE OF THE TRUTH:* What is really right and real? With the Lord Jesus as our perfect pattern, we have the only perfect standard in the world. Jesus said, "I am the Way, the Truth and the Life, no man comes to the Father but by Me." (John 14:6)

(4) *DESIRE TO ACCOMPLISH:* We want our lives to REALLY COUNT. Can we make a mark on history so that people who come after us say, "This man or woman was a credit to their generation?" And what will count more than leading some soul from darkness into light, from the power of Satan to the power of God? All eternity will not erase that work. "And they that be wise shall shine as the brightness of the firmament; and they that turn many to righteousness as the stars, for ever and ever." (Daniel 12:3)

(5) *FREEDOM FROM FEAR:* With an "Eve of Destruction" world around us, Christians can have joy and peace. We *know* the way. We have nothing to be afraid of, in this world or the next. God, the mighty God, is our father. We can have His peace. "Be anxious about *nothing*; but in *everything* by prayer and supplication with thanksgiving let your requests be made known to God; and the peace of God which passes all understanding (and *mis*understanding!)

shall keep your hearts and minds through Christ Jesus."
(Philippians 4:6-7)

(6) *FREEDOM FROM GUILT:* What do you do when you
have done wrong and your mind and heart feel heavy and
depressed? You could try to blot it out with alcohol, put it
down with drugs, shock it deaf by therapy, even try to rap it
out with a psychiatrist. These will help you do one of two
things: Find out *why* you are feeling rotten (as if you didn't
know!) or suppress some of
the *results* of feeling bad. But
only Jesus does the thing that
really needs to be done, and
only *He* has the right to do it.
He removes and wipes out
the CAUSE — by forgiving
us. "If we CONFESS our sins,
He is faithful and just to
FORGIVE us our sins, and to
CLEANSE US from ALL un-
righteousness." (I John 1:9)

(7) *LOVE:* EVERYONE wants to be loved. We want
others to love us and accept us for what we are. Where will
love come from when we are not too lovely? From One
Person at least — from *God.* He loved us so much that He
gave His dearest; Jesus came to die for us. Young and old
people all around the world who are Christians are bound
together with God's love. It's a wonderful worldwide family
like nothing else in the Universe. "Greater love has no man
than this; that a man lay down his life for his friends. You
are my friends if you do whatsoever I command you . . . I in
them, and You in Me, that they may be made perfect in one;
and that the world may know that You have sent Me, and
have loved them as You have loved Me." (John 15:13-14;
17:23)

Now, these are mighty things to think about. And you
have much to think about each day. Will you take time to
build yourself, deep in your soul, a place to think in? You
must have every day, a time of *quietness*, of silence. Our
hurried generation has forgotten what it means to "be still
and know that" God is God.

The Bible has much to say on the art of *waiting on God*. "They that WAIT UPON THE LORD shall renew their strength; they shall mount up with wings as eagles; they shall run and not be weary, they shall walk and not faint." (Isaiah 40:31) "Wait on the Lord; be of good courage and He shall strengthen your heart; wait, I say, on the Lord."

HOW TO RELAX AND BE STILL

All of us need a daily time of silence. People are afraid of silence today. They often have to keep moving, keep acting, keep doing things because they are afraid to listen to the voice of God. But it is this perpetual motion, this business, that stops us from really knowing *ourselves* and really knowing *God*. It was easier in the old days where people had farms or forests, hills and sea to go to alone, just to be with God. Today there are cities, traffic, crowds, and noise. It has become harder to be alone. If you can get to a lovely, quiet hill, or forest, then make it a point to go there alone for some time each day if you can at all make the time. The quietness and peace there will strengthen you for the day and give you an inner calm that stands up under pressure. But if you can't, then do this:

Go somewhere where you can be alone and as *quiet* as possible. If you need to, lie down on your bed and put a pillow over your head to cut off the noise and light. For at least fifteen minutes, don't do *anything*. Don't talk, write, read, or worry over problems or things you could be doing.

Just relax in the Presence of God. Think of yourself as a warm strip of sand being washed by the warm, gentle waves of the love of God. To help you ease your tensions and stiffness, so you can relax more readily, you should practice relaxing your body. As you are lying on a bed, lift each limb one at a time beginning with your legs. Hold it up there.

Think of it turning into a heavy slab of concrete. Let it drop down, like a lump of lead on the bed. Do this with both legs, then with your body, letting your stomach relax the same way. Do it with each arm and finish with your head. You weigh a million pounds. You cannot move a muscle. You are not tense or stiff, just a giant sack of potatoes. You are a rag doll with all the stuffing out of it. Now, just lie there. Think about nothing else but the goodness of God. If you drift off to sleep, your "cat-nap" will leave you refreshed and alert. If you are worried about waking up on time, either set an alarm, or ask the Lord to wake you up. Practice this art of relaxed waiting in the Lord's love every day. It will make your busy times deeply useful and worthwhile.

PRACTICING THE PRESENCE OF GOD

To daily experience God's nearness is a thrilling, life-sustaining happening. Brother Lawrence, a sixteenth-century Christian, wrote a little booklet on this subject which has become a classic. It has a practical approach to experimental Christian living. Here, in his own words is how he came to experience the continual sense of the nearness and reality of God in his daily life:

> "Having found in many books methods of going to God . . . I thought this would puzzle me rather than help what I sought after — nothing but to become wholly God's. This made me resolve to give my all for the ALL; after having given myself WHOLLY to God, I renounced, for the love of Him, EVERY-THING that was not His; and I began to live as if there were none but He and I in the world. I worshipped Him as often as I could, keeping my mind on His holy presence, and recalling it as often as it wandered from the path. I made this my business: To drive away everything that was capable of interrupting my thought of God."

> "When we are faithful to keep ourselves in His holy Presence and set Him always before

us, this not only hinders our offending Him or doing anything that may displease Him, but it begets in us a holy freedom, and, if I may so speak, a FAMILIARITY with God, wherewith to ask, and that successfully, the graces we stand in need of. By oft repeating these acts, they become habitual, and the presence of God is rendered as it were natural to us. May all things praise Him. Amen."

Now, brother Lawrence was a monk. He lived in a place where the chief aim of the whole community was to draw closer to God. But we don't usually have that advantage. We have to know God in the daily rounds of life. Yet we can still know Him like he did. God doesn't want us to think *only* of Him all day. And it is not as though the only time we are really right with Him is when we *consciously* have Him in our minds; that is both impossible and unnecessary. He only wants *FIRST PREFERENCE* in our thoughts and affections; that is what it means to "love God with all your heart and soul and mind and strength."

The following ideas will help you practice His presence:

(a) *Pray "without ceasing."* That is, get into a *habit* of taking every problem, small and great, to the Lord. Ask Him to help clear the telephone lines for you; to help you fix up a car, finish your homework, or get housework done in time. And get into the same habit of *thanking* Him for everything that comes your way.

(b) *Be satisfied only in doing His will.* You will have "gray" days where no sun seems to shine, and God seems a million miles away. But these must be sometimes. Through the times of wind and rain, God teaches us discipline and obedience. Nothing but sunshine makes a desert. A tree that has not learned to bend in the wind cannot stand in a storm. God will test you by taking away the sense of His presence for a while. The question is: Will you still do what is RIGHT even when you don't feel His closeness? You talk about trusting *Him*, but *can He trust you* to be faithful?

(c) Life for you must be a *life of faith*. Don't let routine or organization tie you down. If you can't drop all that you are doing at His command, you are not in the right place with God. Live in such a way as to create a DAILY DEPEN- DENCE on Him. Every Christian must so live as to need God in everything they do. Never insure and insulate yourself so well that you think you have no need to trust Jesus.

(d) *Keep short accounts with God*. If you do something wrong or displeasing to Him, confess it immediately, get it right and receive His forgiveness. Live clean from sin. It is wrong-doing that blocks the sense of His presence more than anything else. Make a habit of asking the Holy Spirit to search your heart every week or so, to make sure that you are both growing in the Lord, and keeping yourself close to His love and light.

(e) Remember: *God's love does not change* according to how much you love Him. He knows who you are and where you are, and He loves you just the same.

BIBLE MEDITATION

Many promises are made in the Scriptures to the person who will *meditate* on the truth of God. Meditation is like thinking God's thoughts after Him; so we begin to think the same way *He* does about things, and can speak to Him in His own language and with His own ideas. When we think over Scripture deeply, we are learning how to express our own thoughts and feelings in Biblical ways to our world and to God. If we will meditate on God's word, we will have these promises for *success* (Joshua 1:8); *satisfaction and joy* (Psalms 63:5-6); *understanding* (Psalms 119:99); *boldness* (Psalms 119:46-48); *courage* (Psalms 119:92-93); *prosperity* (Psalms 1:1-3; and *faith* (Romans 10:17).

Now the way to meditate properly on Scripture is to THINK about each one, part by part. Just take one verse at a time. Ask yourself, "*What* is being said? *Where* is it being said? *Who* is saying it? *How* is he saying it? *When* is it being said? "Keep asking *questions* about it. Find out if it is a promise, a warning, a direction, or a command. If it is a *promise*, ask yourself what are its conditions; who is making it; when it can be claimed; and who can claim it? If it is a warning, ask yourself who does it apply to, why is it here, and what does it tell me? If a *direction*, what does it say to do, and what does it say will be the result? If it is a *command*, ask the same questions. Then *write out* what you find if you like, and think about it. Put it in your notebook for Bible study, and/or write the verse out on a card for memorization. Carry it in your heart. In this way, you will learn to "hide the Word of God in your heart" so you will be kept close to God and far from sin.

The best way to meditate on verses of scripture is to take life situations that you experience and find out what God has to say about them. If you have a problem or a need, look it up in the Bible, and write out all the verses you can find on the subject. Then *think through* each one. Use study tools like a concordance and a dictionary to help you find the meanings

of words and how they apply. Then start thinking about how you can use each verse in your life. What will it mean to ACT on the conditions or directions of the verse you are thinking about? How can you DO what the verse says to do? What kind of situation can be covered by the warning or the promise you are thinking about? As you take time to think through God's Word, using the tool of meditation, you will find your life growing in power, authority, and depth with God.

III

THE STUDY: Training

Along this corridor, there is a little room that unfortunately doesn't get as much use as it could in the house of your life. It's the STUDY, the place where you learn to love God with all your MIND. Let's take a look inside!

MAKING THE MOST OF YOUR STUDY TIME

"You are the light of the world. A city that is set on a hill cannot be hid." That's what Jesus said about His people. Now if an angel came into your classes at school and asked the sinners there who the Christians were, would they point to you? Do your friends at school know that you love Jesus? Do your teachers? Do your studies show it?

Every school needs Christians. There are a lot of things that you can use later in the service of God if you do your work well. *Languages* will be useful if you witness in another country. *Social studies* will help you know how people live in other lands. *Sciences* will help train you to think clearly and test out what you believe. Classes in *English, speech,* and *drama* will show you how to speak and write so that people will listen to you. *History* is a lesson in what happens to nations that honor or forget God. *Biology* will help you see what wonderful creatures God made and give you opportunities to present the Biblical picture of creation.

Of course, many of your teachers will not know Jesus. Most books you are given to read will not discuss Him. Many subjects at school will be given to you as if God had nothing to say about them at all. But you don't have to be afraid that these will make you lose your faith. If you will think harder, and spend more time asking questions of Christian friends, you will find your faith comes out stronger. *God* is not afraid of "being proved wrong." You will find that true faith really makes more sense than no faith at all, and you will learn how to speak up for Jesus in a world that does not like to serve or love Him. What *better* place to learn that at school?

You do not have to go to another land to be a missionary. Your *school* probably has more people who don't know Jesus per square INCH than "heathen" lands have per square ACRE of jungle. You don't become a missionary by crossing the sea, but by seeing the cross! Every person who knows and loves Jesus is called to be a missionary, and every person who does not, is his or her mission field. Your school needs Jesus very much.

Do these things if you want to count for Christ. Take your studies to God. Treat each class like an assignment from Jesus to witness. Ask God, "How can I speak for you in this class Lord?" Look hard at the homework and reports you must make for each class. Let God open your mind as to how they can be used as a tool for getting out 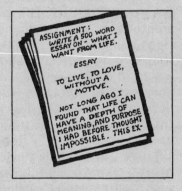 the Good News to both the other kids and your teacher. Think of the classes where you can speak or write for Him! Consider English (essays, free verse, poetry); or speech (how problems of the world might be met by Jesus or Christian people); history (how God's people affected it for good); art (pictures and posters that can preach) and others. And do your homework wisely and well. Be a person kids can go to for help.

Win their respect and your teacher's too, by doing your work neatly, well, and for Jesus' sake. Don't be phony or try too hard. Just be relaxed, happy in God, and show, by your balance and friendliness, that you have found something in Someone who has helped you in all areas of your life.

Have you let God use *your* studies as a channel of witness? If you have been hung up on various problems of the past, you no doubt have completely blown many opportunities to do anything worthwhile in study for Christ. But perhaps it is not too late. Perhaps you can begin again and try to recapture some lost ground. And if there is any improvement at all, you can use even *this* little gain as a witness to the real change Jesus brings in a life. Here are some simple guidelines to help you make the most of your study time and organize it to the best advantage:

(1) Have a *SPECIAL PLACE* set aside for your study. Explain to your family or household your need for quietness and privacy there. Make it *good to go to*; have any drawing tools, reference books, charts, and texts on hand. Set up a good BRIGHT LIGHT to illuminate your work comfortably without dimness or glare. The best form of light is INDIRECT, DIFFUSED and electric. It should not throw a shadow on your desk, nor shine in your eyes. If you can't get a desk light, move your desk to the best place you can under your room's roof light. Change the bulb if it isn't bright enough. When you make notes, your textbook and notebook should be *evenly lit* to help you avoid eyestrain.

(2) Set a *TIME LIMIT* on your study. Prepare before hand, begin on time, and work as rapidly and as thoroughly as possible on the subject. DON'T ALLOW DISTRACTIONS (phone calls, radio, visitors)! CONCENTRATE. Work against the clock. Stop on time. Don't study if you are too tired; the work will be ineffective.

(3) *VARY* your studying time. If you are working for a couple of hours on one thing, break it up into smaller lots. If you start making a lot of mistakes, do something else, and come back to that problem later. Your subconscious mind will have a little time to work on it, and it may come out better for you later. If you have to work late, and you start to get tired, do something DIFFERENT — take a SHORT snack, go for a run outside, do some push-ups! You can do this also when you want to start on a new subject, as the one you have just finished will still be on your mind.

(4) *PLAN A STUDY GUIDE*. Timetable the amount of work you have to get through. Divide your time fairly EVENLY between subjects, but with a little more emphasis on those that you find tougher. Do it neatly, and PIN IT UP where you can see it constantly as a reminder. It should be FLEXIBLE to allow some changes, but on the whole, after you've made it, STICK TO IT. Work UNDER PRESSURE; it is better for you to do a good, solid, intense hour of study, and then take a couple of hours off doing something else, than to fritter away three hours fooling around half-heartedly at one subject. DISCIPLINE is something you must learn from the Holy Spirit. Learn to pace yourself against yourself. COMMIT each session to the Lord. Ask for guidance as to the amount of time you spend on each section. Don't wait for the right "mood" to study; just begin anyway.

LEARNING: You need a CHALLENGE to give you incentive.

TESTS or *EXAMS* are never very far away! Consistent study throughout the year pays off; try counting the weeks or days before set tests or exams start to "spark" you. Your *WITNESS* in exams is vital. How is it that you can be calm, confident, and cheerful? Your unsaved friends will want to know. How can you keep relaxed under the pressure of tough tests and exams? The answer: Christ; and a sharp study program that keeps you on top. If you fool around and fail, your witness in this field is finished. Your study could be a help towards determining THEIR DESTINY. Your witness is very important in studies. For Jesus' sake, don't fool around.

CRITICIZE material you read and hear — don't drink in everything without thinking! The evolution theory is an example of a field of study where you can present an effective testimony. Asking yourself *questions* will help you grasp the key thought behind the material better. Try to develop a real INTEREST in the subject; think of it in terms of how it could help you in God's work later on. Keep this goal in mind as you study.

WITNESSING TO YOUR TEACHERS

"He (Jesus) was sitting among the teachers. He was *hearing* what they said and *asking questions*. All those who heard Him were surprised and wondered about His understanding and what He said." (Luke 2:46-47)

Your *teachers*, too, need Jesus. Some of them have problems that only He can take care of. They may seem touchy or mad because of problems that make them feel hurt or lonely. Your teachers ARE really just people! Think about that for a while. And people have problems, sometimes bigger than themselves. You don't know as much as they do in many things, but you *do* know the Lord Jesus. Study what He did to witness to teachers.

Jesus both *LISTENED AND ASKED QUESTIONS*. Teachers respected what He said because of the questions He asked. This is the way to witness to teachers. Your questions should show them you understand some things that not many people understand. This means you must show *respect* and *honor* for your teachers. Jesus did. How is YOUR attitude towards them? It is possible to be right and say the right things in the wrong way. We are not to try to do God's work in the Devil's spirit. Don't be a smart alec. Don't disobey God by acting as if your teacher is an absolute idiot in everything just because you disagree with him or because he doesn't know the Lord. You are not a know-it-all; don't act like one. If you have an argumentative, critical spirit, you will deserve it if your teacher makes you look like a fool in class.

Make sure of your facts. Take time to get good ones. If you know you are going to get into a subject where you will have to speak up for Jesus, get ready early. Read up on it from some good Christian books that your pastor or Christian bookseller can recommend. Have the facts, from the Christian point of view, at hand. Wait and pray for a chance to put in your word for the Lord. You don't have to be bossy when you do this. Say something like, "Dr. X is one of the top men in his field, and *he* has quite a different view. He says . . ."

This means you will *not* speak out strongly unless you are very sure of your facts. It is wise to say, "I may be *wrong*, but I thought that . . ." Or, "Isn't there another side to this question?" Much harm can be done to the cause of Christ if you come on too strongly with something that turns out to be wrong. Have your facts backed up by reliable sources. The Bible says, "*Prove* all things. Hold fast to that which is good." (I Thessalonians 5:21)

You must *EARN* the right to be heard. Make the class WANT to believe you by being the kind of person they can look up to. Always be kind. There is no excuse for a follower of Jesus to be biting or critical. God's Word tells us to "speak the truth in love." If you get some facts that really put down something a teacher said, make it easy for him to back down. Give him the benefit of the doubt. Resist the temptation to make him look like a fool in the eyes of the class. Say, "I may have gotten the wrong idea on what you said before; but I found this that says this . . . You didn't mean THAT did you?"

Loan good books to your teacher that will help explain your stand. Ask older Christians for their advice on what to give him or her. Ask your teacher for his opinion of the book by challenging him (in a nice way) to read it. You could say, "Here is a book that makes some valid points on the opposite side of what you discussed with us in class. How would you react to what this man has written?" If a local resident or someone who visits your town can factually and intelligently present the Christian position on a subject, ask the teacher if he could arrange to have that person share his views to the class one period. Ask him if he would like to hear another view. Be honest about this. Do not lie or pretend just to get someone in to "preach" or you may get your teacher into trouble; and he may hate you for it besides killing any future chances for a Christian witness in your school. Be ready to help in any way you can. And tell him you are praying for him. Then you DO just that. He may be won to Jesus by your witness. It has happened before.

HOW TO MEMORIZE MATERIAL BETTER

Want to remember better? You too, can have an "adding-machine" memory! There are three parts to your memory: LEARNING, RETENTION, and RECALL:

(1) *LEARNING:* "Feeding-in" information. Practice the following:

(a) Use your senses — as many as you can (eyes, ears, touch, "muscle memory"). The best way to memorize is to WRITE OUT and/or CARTOON the material, and READ IT ALOUD at the same time. Use every memory input you can.

(b) Don't try for too long. Don't be fooled that you are "remembering" when you let your eyes keep skipping over the same words. Short, sharp, strict times are best.

(c) Learn to CONCENTRATE. Ask God to help strengthen your willpower.

(d) Memorize AS A WHOLE. You will find it better in the long run to study large portions of connected things as one unit. You will see less immediate results than when you learn "bits"; but it is better in the long run. Learn a POEM, for instance, by reading the *whole thing* through each study time; don't try to break it up. The relationship between parts will help you remember.

(e) *RECITE* material (without notes) after learning it. You will be able to see how much you have really learned. Repeat this often. Set yourself "spot tests" in text conditions.

(f) If you have any talent for *drawing* or *cartooning*, try to put things like history and time charts into *line drawings* and *pictures*. It is easier to remember *pictures* than *words*. Don't be afraid to make your pictures look weird or funny. If you can get *variety* and *color, brightness* and *unusualness* into your cartoons, you will add even more to the chances of learning the material. Put long sequences of events into simple "codes" by making up silly sentences of key words or key ideas, and learn these. Associate ideas with concrete objects, like making a picture of a fountain pen to help you remember William Penn. All you really need to help you remember is a good imagination. *REMEMBER:* The *funnier* or *stranger* you can make your memory helps, the EASIER it will be to remember them.

(2) *RETENTION:* "Over-learning." CARRY ON after you feel you have learned it "perfectly just a few more

times. This extra effort makes results far more lasting. SPACE your learning time out well. An hour a day, not a seven-hour learning session! Remember too, you can ask the Lord to help you retain what you have learned. Don't worry that you may forget it all; it is often worry itself that blocks out your thinking! Most of it will come back right on time, if you have carefully followed these suggestions. It may help you to put your summaries, cartoon charts, etc. on *pieces of cards*, and carry them with you during the day. At odd moments, you can just thumb through them, and test yourself. Put the full "translation" of your memory help on *one* side, then just enough of the help or question on the *other* side to begin your recall process. Use these often.

(3) *RECALL: Getting back* that memorized material!

(a) *Again, don't be afraid* you might forget or that very fear will make you do just that! Put your trust in the Lord, and you will go in to your test better prepared and more relaxed.

(b) If you can't recall immediately, WAIT A WHILE. Do something else and return to the problem later. A quick prayer will help. When you get back to it, it may have worked itself out already. If you have carried something in your head that you see is needed on first glance through the paper, write it out immediately on a sheet of scrap paper for later use. This lets you clear your head of the things that you were worried you might forget.

(c) Be CONFIDENT that you will be able to recall what you need. And don't worry if you can't; just say, "Praise the Lord" anyway and go on to something else. Worry will only cloud your memory and cause you to forget more than you already have.

One last word of advice: Don't try to learn EVERY-THING; stick with just the ESSENTIALS.

TIPS FOR TAKING NOTES

The WAY you take notes could be the reason that "cramming" is hard for you. Here are some ideas that will help you take notes you can be envied for — and that will be a real blessing to you when the studying gets tough:

(1) *Take PRIDE in your notebooks.* If possible PRINT or TYPE up key sections, although the latter uses time that you may not have. Even in the retyping of class notes, you will be helping your mind to memorize what you have learned. *Messy* notes are hard to study from, and it's depressing to try. Use sharp pencils, ruled lines, and good strong inks.

(2) *Use your imagination* when you take notes. Look for *similarities* in letters and definitions that will help you associate and remember better, for example:
Para-magnetic - *P*ulls away from the field
Dia -magnetic - *D*raws into the field.

(3) *Change your LETTER SIZES for emphasis.* Try a *COLOR CODE.* You can use a different colored pencil or felt pens for this. *BLACK:* Important formula or phrases; *RED:* Key words or concepts; *GREEN:* Important fact or measurement. As you take notes, if you have time, change your colors when you write. It will make your notes brighter, and easier to read, and to remember.

(4) Leave *WIDE MARGINS* to summarize material into small key phrases. Draw ARROWS into formulas or definitions to draw attention to them in revision; STARS (*) for important points; "N. B." for things you have been asked to pay special attention to. Write KEY WORDS out in the margin beside the passage in which they occur for quick reference later.

(5) *NUMBER* your pages and make an *INDEX*. Use this as a check list when you study. When you are reviewing for

tests, concentrate on the emphasized parts, those colored or written down in large print. This way you spend more time on the necessary parts.

YOU CAN READ WITH A LOT MORE SPEED

And that has nothing at all to do with drugs! A novel in 30 minutes flat? *Dr. Zhivago* or *War and Peace* in a day? Maybe you won't be *that* good, but here are some tips to push your reading rate up a few notches:

In your spare time, give yourself a reading-speed test. Use a simple story-type book on something you would like, but neither too dull or too interesting subject matter. As a model of simplicity and style, something like *The Pearl* by John Steinbeck or *The Old Man and the Sea* by Ernest Heminway are good examples. Set a time limit of *one minute* by either using a kitchen timer or having a friend time you with a sweep-second hand. Read at your normal "pleasure-reading" speed. Stop on time, and count the number of words. *Results: Below* 300 words — poor; 300-349 — fair; 350-399 — good; over 399 — excellent.

IMPROVING YOUR READING RATE: If you were a little slow, here's what to do:

(1) *DON'T READ ALOUD.* Put your finger on your lips while reading; there should be no movement. Break yourself of the unconscious habit of reading aloud under your breath.

(2) *Concentrate on the MEANINGS* of GROUPS of words, not on the words themselves. Just go through, trying to pick up the CONTENT of what is happening, and don't get hung up on admiring the shape of each letter.

(3) *Go for ESSENTIALS only.* Your eyes do NOT move steadily along the line of print, but "jump" from group to group. If you read, looking for a special group of words or a key paragraph, you can sometimes grasp up to three lines in one "jump" just by flicking your eyes from section to section, just touching on essentials.

(4) Read the next passage, but this time *PUSH* yourself. Don't dwell on words "chewing" them over — just blaze on rapidly, picking out only the key words in the material. Retime yourself. Do this often. You will find that you can sometimes *double* your rate. We all actually "see" words faster than our brains can begin to grasp them. By better concentration and alertness, we can begin to use our eyes like two fast cameras, "shooting" everything on a page in a very rapid scan.

To SCAN: Sometimes you aren't going to seriously study any book at all; you are either just trying to learn what it's generally about, or you are looking for some important point in the text. "Scanning" will help. To "scan" a book for its general content, first read any index or chapters it has by titles only. Then just flip through it, letting your eyes drift from section to section, pausing only on brief paragraphs and ends of chapters. Push on quickly; don't dawdle. If you are looking for a key word or paragraph; FIX CLEARLY in your mind the *exact word* you are looking for; then "sweep" the lines as quickly as you possibly can; concentrating ONLY for that word. Your eyes will hit it, and because your mind is carrying a picture of the word it will "home in" the second your eyes cut past it. In this way, you can sometimes "scan" a page every *three seconds!* Speed-reading is never the best for solid material that takes a lot of concentrated throught or for memory work; but by practice, you can even speed up somewhat your ability to comprehend what you are reading faster. Don't you *DARE* use this idea on your Bible readings for personal worship and devotion! But faster reading will save you a lot of time in outlining material, getting rough ideas of plots, and increasing your knowledge of different subjects through wider reading.

Well, there you are, Einstein! All you have to do now is USE these things in that "room" of yours and watch your teachers' eyes pop as you go for the top! Above all, make sure you have your heart and head ready to serve Jesus when He gives you the green light to speak out for Him in class. Ask God for the gift of Divine wisdom. James 3:13-18 tells what it is like: "Who among you is wise and understands? Let that one show from a good life by the things he does that he is wise and gentle . . . the wisdom that comes from Heaven is first of all pure. Then it gives peace. It is gentle and willing to obey. It is full of loving-kindness and of doing good. It has no selfish doubts and does not pretend to be something it is not. Those who plant seeds of peace will gather what is right and good."

HELPFUL SCRIPTURES FOR YOU

God's study-help promises: James 1:5; John 6:13; John 14:13, 26; Proverbs 2:6; 22:17.

Our part in study at school: Colossians 3:23-24; I Thessalonians 5:21; Proverbs 9:9, 10.

For "examinitis": Isaiah 26:3; 12:2; 33:6; Proverbs 3:5, 6

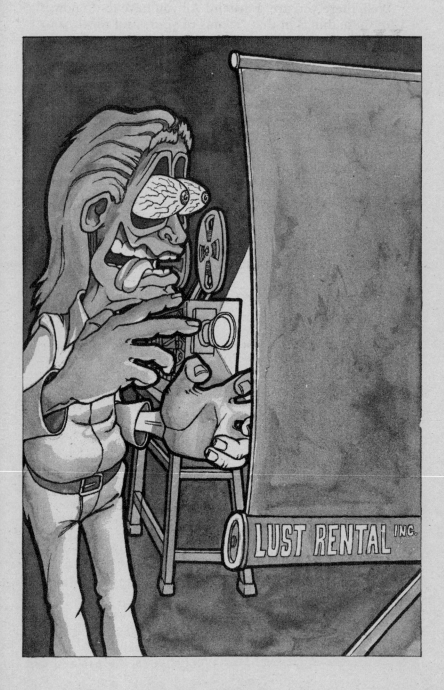

IV

THE LIBRARY: Thoughts

Here is the room where you keep a record of all your thoughts of all the things you have done. It's the LIBRARY where all the books of your thoughts are kept. Let's take a look at some of the shelves and see what kind of volumes you keep here.

THE INVADERS OF THE MIND

There is a battle on today at this very moment — not with bombs or bullets, tanks or rockets — but a very real war all the same. It is a battle for your *mind*. That battle is being carried out by a hundred different people and groups who are all competing for control of your head. Some want it for power or personal gain. Some who launch the attack are backed by the powers of the *pit* itself. That battle is on each time you listen to a record, turn on the radio, watch T.V., read a book, magazine or comic, or see a film. Whoever gains control of your mind has the citadel of your soul. If you lose the battle for your mind, you will begin the battle of wrong deeds and habits. The quickest, safest way to stay out of trouble is to win the first war and learn how to beat the invaders of the mind.

DON'T LET THE MEDIA BE YOUR MASTER

Now whether you are tempted or not can have much to do with what you allow to reach your mind. It is not by accident that you stock your library shelves with books that are cynical, immoral, or low-level literature. The books you *like* to read tell the world a great deal about the kind of person you really are. Nor is it an accident that you have a collection of hard or acid-rock records to feed your record player. What channels are tuned in on your home or car radio? What programs do you really most enjoy watching on T.V.? Most especially we must watch the media around us.

MUSIC is one force that has great power to affect our minds. It is easy to feel afraid when someone plays spooky music on a dark night. A happy song in the same place can change the whole atmosphere and make the room seem different. Music is a message in itself, and because it is a chief tool of some brainraiders, you must be careful to listen only for the glory of God.

Stay away from places where there will be music loud or freaky enough to bend your head. Stay away from any media you have no control over. If you let yourself get into a place where something begins to have power over you, you have gotten away from Jesus. *There are three kinds of dangerous sound* that mark music Satan can use. Avoid listening to these at all costs. Never expose yourself deliberately to them, especially at high volume levels;  never use them for "entertainment" or to fill your home. THE ONE MAJOR THING A CHRISTIAN YOUNG

PERSON MUST DO TODAY IS TO GUARD HIS HEART FROM THE MUSIC OF HELL. There is an old story about Greek sailors who sailed past the Island of Circe. There, a race of enchantresses sang powerfully sweet, drawing songs. But the mariners who listened to the Sirens of Circe were dashed to bits on the rocks around the island. The song they sang was a song of death. And from an international rock brotherhood, kids by the millions are being told what to do and how to do it by "D. J. priests" and "rock-artist preachers" in the revolutionary religion of electric sound. Here are the three forms of sound you should avoid. They will be dangerous to your life in Jesus. They can plant hidden time bombs that will detonate in doubt and destruction later in life. Avoid them at all costs. Remember the sirens of Circe.

(1) *The BLUE NOTE/MINOR* key combination is the least harmful of these three types of sound. It is "downer" music; it can make you feel sad, empty and lonely. It is a suicidal sound. Now some Christians can use this sort of sound to sing Christian songs. It can be used to describe trouble or problems life has; it can describe the past life of sin. But it never ought to be the basic sound of Christians. The Lord Jesus told us to "rejoice" in trouble, not to complain or moan about it. He even went to the cross for the "joy that was set before him." (Luke 6:23; 2 Corinthians 7:4; Hebrews 12:2) If sad music takes a big place in our musical tastes, there may be something wrong with our souls. Sadness is not the mark of a Christian. Minor music must take a minor place.

(2) *The HIGH-ENERGY, BODY-PULSED BEAT:* This is the "heartbeat of Hell"; the most dangerous form of non-Christian sound; it is commonly called "hard-rock." It is dangerous for two reasons: It can damage your peace; and it can teach your body to control your mind. The pulse-beat sound is not new; men have used it for thousands of years to psyche themselves up for love or war or pleasure. Today, it is usually created by the electronic bass and percussion sections. It is sound pulsed into the basic, primal rhythms of your body. It is dangerous because it is so exciting that you can let it control your soul.

Some groups are masters of the "primal pulse." Many of them know how to build intense energy into their music. It can hook like a drug. It must be learned. It grows on you. Play hard rock to a baby and it will probably cry. Play it to a little kid and he may not like it at all — the first time. But keep on playing that same sound a little at a time, and he will *learn* to like it. If that baby becomes a teenager, growing under that sound, he will later have to *force* himself to stop from moving with it.

One manager of a top U. S. rock band, a political activist, has this to say about his music:

> "Our program is *cultural revolution* through a total assault . . . which makes use of every tool, every energy, and every media we can get our hands on. We breathe revolution. We will do anything to drive people crazy out of their heads and into their bodies. Rock . . . is the spearhead of our attack, because it is effective and so much fun. We have developed organic, high-energy guerrilla bands who are infiltrating the popular culture and destroying millions of minds in the process . . . You don't need to get rid of the honkies. You just ROB THEM OF THEIR REPLACEMENTS . . . We don't have guns yet — not all of us anyway. We have more powerful weapons. DIRECT ACCESS to the minds of millions of teenagers is one of our most potent, and THEIR BELIEF IN US is another."

God says, "Don't let the world force you into its model. Be a unique person in the manner of your actions and thoughts." (Romans 12:1, 2)

(3) DISTORTION & PSYCHEDELICS, commonly called "ACID ROCK": Acid music was introduced through the drug culture. It was made possible by the mastering of electronics in sound, by new deliberate distortion, rerecording techniques and special attachments to guitars and amplifiers. In acid rock, sound is bent, twisted, distorted, and rechanneled through the senses. Regular timings and rhythms are upset and forced into dissonant and unpredictable patterns. Psychedelic sound was first popularized by the Beatles in their *Revolver* album, with the song "Tomorrow Never Knows." They used it again in *Sergeant Pepper*, and others began to build a new era in rock with it. Jimi Hendrix, Eric Clapton and other masters of the guitar extended the acid sound into complex levels of antimusic musical genius. It became the mark of the turned-on generation.

But no one can listen long to acid rock without some form of spiritual damage. Psychedelic sound IS spirit music; but it has a *different* spirit and a *different* sound from the songs sung in heaven. Acid rock can play havoc with the soul. It can create fear, unrest, and tension. It is an accurate reflection of the loneliness, chaos, and madness of our world — of the mystic spirit-worlds of Satan trying to break into man's being. But it is sound which opens the door of the mind to occult attack. Satan's game is with the *mind*, and this is illusion music. It not only recreates drug trips, it creates its *own* trips, into the dark world of the Enemy. This is not the sound heard "near to the heart of God." This is not the music of the Good Shepherd who leads beside the still waters. No angel from the realms of glory ever used *this* sound to announce the birth of the

Messiah. But it is possible that acid sounds will usher in a "new Jesus" to a world of waiting, deceived disciples who have sold out their souls to the worship of their generation's music. And only the informed Christian will know the real Jesus well enough to stay away from it.

IDEAS IN MUSIC

Now it is important that Christians stay in touch with what is happening around them. We must retain our sense of what the world is like, so we will know how to reach it for Jesus. We are IN the world, but we are not to be LIKE it. Jesus said to His Father, "I have given Your Word to My followers. The world hated them because they do not belong to the world even as I do not belong to the world. I do not ask you to take them out of the world. I ask You to keep them from the Devil." (John 17:14-15) We are to live holy lives, but not be hermits. Living in a *hole* will not make us holy! We must know what the world is doing so we can speak in the language they will understand when we speak for God and right. But there are some things we must watch. The ideas which worldly songs get across can stick in our minds. If we are not careful, we will mix these into our Christian thinking. Worse still, we may come to think that is the way things really are and accept wrong things as right.

You have all heard ideas like, "No adult understands young people"; "Old people never know where it's at"; "Never trust anyone over thirty." Scores of songs over the past ten years have sold this idea. Bob Dylan's song "Times Are A Changin'" was one of the first with its "Come mothers and fathers throughout the land; and don't criticize what you can't understand." Of course, there are a lot of adults who don't know where it's at. But there are just as many kids with the same problem. The Bible tells us to respect the advice of the old and not put them down. Some of us may even live to be over thirty ourselves. *Then* what will we say to our kids?

The "Now" ethic says that only *today* is important, that we should forget the past, and no one needs to think about history. Many songs have wiped out faith that there WILL be any future, starting far back with songs like Barry McGuire's giant hit "Eve of Destruction." A lot of kids do not care about the past. Yet if we don't learn from it, we will make the same mistakes people made before us. History is important. The BIBLE is a history book. The future also means something to the Christian. God has a "new world coming." Christians will have new bodies. We are not to worry about the future, but we are to "lay up for ourselves treasures in Heaven."

Other song ideas will hurt our thought-life. The media is filled with music that says, in so many words, that sex outside of God's laws is natural and fun; that drugs are acceptable means of reaching reality; that all adults are hypocrites; that God is rather irrelevant or Jesus was nothing much more than a misguided, middle-aged hippie. Even when songs are *about* Jesus, we must think and check it carefully against the Bible. All songs about Jesus or God may not be about the RIGHT Jesus or God. The real Jesus said, "Be careful that no one leads you the wrong way. Many people will come *using My name* . . . they will fool many people and turn them the wrong way." (Matthew 24:4-5)

I'll say it again: The CHIEF DANGER A YOUNG CHRISTIAN PERSON WILL HAVE WILL COME FROM HIS OR HER *MUSIC*. Guard your mind by guarding your ears. Don't spend God's money on the devils' messages, no matter how attractively they are packaged.

CHRISTIAN MUSIC: WHAT IS IT?

Are there any rules for Christian music? Can we say anything about a sound that will be marked in any generation or any culture as Christian? Many say this is not possible; that all we can really say in any generation is that music should *conform to reality* and should be true to what actually is. This means that we have no guidelines in writing sounds that will be of honor to God; because Christ is Lord of all, anything at all can be used, including the hard and the acid sounds generated by the subculture in the early sixties.

But is this true? We know this about truth that will help us decide: If something is Biblically true, it will always apply in every culture, at every time in history, in its basic principles. And while it is difficult to define the actual structure or chording, or the harmony and consonance of a sound which will honor God, the Bible has not left us without guidelines.

All Biblical music is music of worship. There is fundamentally no other form in Scripture. Worship can be generated from only two ultimate bases: A supreme regard for the glory of God, or an ultimate preference for ourselves. Music is a mobilization of the power of worship. And a principle we can analyze music by is this: What is its motive? Is it self or God-centered? Does it point to man or to God? Is it the music of love or the music of selfishness? To find this we can look at I Corinthians 13 again and ask ourselves —

WHAT DOES THE MUSIC OF LOVE SOUND LIKE?

(a) *Love's music is PATIENT:* People resist change. Each new sound in Christian history has been firmly resisted by the back-slidden dropouts of the previous awakening — and if new forms of music are brought to the church, they cannot be forced. Is *your* music patient? Music that demands its own way is not love's sound; love challenges without forcing.

(b) *Love's music is KIND:* It is not bitter or hostile, violent or vicious. In Romans, chapter one, Paul lists the characteristics of a society that has heart-rejected God; the end result of such a world is people without natural affection, without pity or mercy. Love's music is not ruthless; kindness is goodness and graciousness which gently breaks down resistance. The end of the music of hardness is a calloused conscience; does your music reflect kindness?

(c) *Love's music is not ENVIOUS:* It has no desire to copy or emulate the gods of a pagan world. Music can be a prop for acceptance; if it is your "whole life," it is not enough! Groups that sing and play must ask themselves this: "Is this the overflow of my love and gratitude to God?" A music which seeks recognition is not a ministry, but a mission field.

(d) *Love's music is not PROUD:* It does not show off. It is not driven by desire to push its sound, its group, its talent. Love's music knows who it is; it doesn't have to talk itself up or talk itself down. It doesn't think much about itself at all; but its object is love; its focus is worship. Is that the Lord Jesus? Is that *Him?* Who do people think about when they hear your kind of sound? We must know the difference between vision and ambition.

(e) *Love's music doesn't MISBEHAVE:* It does nothing deliberately to offend. Posture, display and affectation have no place in the music of God. It is not rude, unmannerly, or indecent. The Greek word "hyperion" means "actor" — and is the word the New Testament translates in English as "hypocrite." In our quest for spiritual reality — are we real? For music to be a genuine expression of a life-style, there must be no acting. Your true self will be revealed in the music you delight in; what kind of person do you show the world?

(f) *Love doesn't SEEK HER OWN:* Self-centered music is reflected from self-centered living. The world is polarizing into two groups who earn respect; the vile and the virtuous; the man who wants to walk between will never change it. Love doesn't seek its own way, insist on its own rights, or chase rainbows that were never generated by the Son.

(g) *Love's music is NOT EASILY PROVOKED:* Christian music is not reaction, but action. All of God's decisions come from the internal pressure of His wisdom and love; none come from external pressures or problems. Too much music is written in reaction; "Here is what people think or do; I'll write something relevant against it." But love isn't pushed into reply. Love generates her sound from the loveliness of her Lover; it keeps no score of wrongs.

(h) *Love THINKS NO EVIL:* There is great pressure in the world of ideas. We must not give in to secular concepts; we must not surrender to the pressure of society. Remember this fundamental fact — the world is always wrong. According to the Bible, the world is forever against the true Church; and it will only court her to try to ~~rape her and~~ *steal*

—45—

murder her. Any passing interest it displays will always prove shallow, self-centered and short-lived.

(i) *Love's music DOES NOT REJOICE IN INIQUITY:* It finds no happiness in sin. Love's music will not glorify or magnify rottenness; no major time will be spent on the wrongness of the world; gloating over others' sin; being glad when people go wrong. When it touches sin, it will do so as God does — in sadness, in holy hatred, in judgment — and in brief.

(j) *Love's music REJOICES IN TRUTH:* This is her joy and delight — the truth of God; not just what He *does*, but Who He *IS*. All Biblical music can be tested ultimately by this; does it center its excitement around God? Does it worship in "spirit and in truth"? (John 4:23-24) This tells us two things about the music of love: (1) It has a genuine *truth content*. It must be real and Biblical; it must be filled with the great thoughts of the Word of God. It is this, more than anything else that will focus the sound on reality, turn sentiment into love, add power to sweetness. Is your music real? Do you live constantly in the thoughts of God? (2) *It must be joyous*, even in sadness. There is no Biblical precedent for hopelessness in worship; love's music has unquenchable faith; limitless vision; eagerness to dare for the best because of the greatness of her Lord. *The cross is a positive sign*. It was for the "joy that was set before Him" that the Son of God gave Himself in agony for the sins of the world. Love's music isn't minor; it majors on the power and the glory of the great God.

This must be the firm resolution of our hearts: To reject from our worship, music that does not conform to the gentle criteria of charity, the agapé love of the Bible. *Worship* is the sole function of music in Scripture and *love* is the only motive the Word of God will allow for those that represent the Son. And will it touch the world with power? Will it reach out to those that do not know Him, speaking a language that is strange in their ears? Can such music really be used for anything else other than people who love and enjoy God?

"I have given them Your Word; and the world has hated them, because they are not of this world, even as I am not of this world. I pray not that you should take them out of the world, but that you should keep them from the evil; they are *not of this world*, even as I am not of the world. Make them holy *by the truth*; as you have sent Me into the world, even so have I also sent them into the world. And for their sakes, I set Myself apart, that they may be thoroughly dedicated in the truth."

"But I am not thinking of them only; but I pray for them also which *shall believe on Me through their word*; that they may all be one; as You, Father are in union with Me; and I am in union with You, let them be in union with us that the world may believe that You have sent Me; and the glory which You gave me, *I have given them;* that they may be *one*, even as We are One; I in them and You in Me, that they may be made perfect in one and that *the world may know* that You have sent Me and have loved them, as You have loved Me."

(John 17:14-23, Combined Trans.)

ARE THOUGHTS SIN?

Now it is not thoughts alone that make a person do wrong. Thoughts are just the first step in temptation. And temptation is not sin. The Bible says, "You have never been tempted to sin in any different way than other people. God is faithful. He will not allow you to be tempted more than you can take. But when you are tempted, He will make a way for you to keep from falling into sin." (I Corinthians 10:13)

Why can *Christians* still be tempted? As long as we are able to do right, we are also able to do wrong. No one can be *good* unless they are also able to be bad if they want to. Think of a talking doll. Pull the string in her back and she says,

"Hello!" Pull it again, and she says something else. She will say whatever she was *made* to say. Now God could have made us like talking dolls, so that when He pulled a string we said to Him, "I love you." But would it REALLY be love?

To be free to obey Him, we also have to be free to disobey Him. God is looking for people He can trust. We talk about trusting Him, but can He trust us? He cannot have people in His new world that want to give in to sin. This life is our testing time. If we really love Him, we will not give in to sin. If tests come, we must learn to lean on God and be strong in His power. Tests only prove what our hearts are like.

Now, to be *tempted* is not *sin*. Temptation is just an idea or feeling put to your mind or body that you know you must not give in to. It is a suggestion to gratify some desire in an illegal way or amount. But you can have a very strong temptation; REFUSE IT, and stay just as holy and clean as Jesus did. Temptation only becomes sin when you *give in* to it. James says, "When you are tempted to do wrong, don't say 'God is tempting me!' He will never tempt anyone, and He Himself cannot be tempted. A man is tempted to do wrong when he lets himself be led by what his bad thoughts tell him to do. When he *does* what his bad thoughts tell him to do, he sins."

Now, temptation can come from *three main places*. Jesus was tempted in all these ways, but He never gave in to sin.

(A) Temptation can come from *worldly people* around us. Old friends can try to pull us back to our old way of life. The Bible calls this tempting crowd "the world." Satan said to Jesus in the desert, "I will give you all this power and greatness. It has been given to me; if you worship *me*, it will be yours." But Jesus refused. You never have to give in to the tug of a wrong crowd. No matter how strong the pressure is, it is better to get out than to give in. (Luke 4:6-7)

(B) Temptation can also come from our *old memories*, from habits we used to have when we lived in sin. God cannot just "wipe out" our old memories because they are the only record we have of who we ARE: they are a real part of us. But He has a better way to deal with our past. When old thoughts or feelings come back to bother us, we must use these as a SIGNAL to turn again IMMEDIATELY to Jesus. We will find *in Him* all we need. If we are lonely, we can ask Him to show Himself to us as the Great Friend who sticks "closer than a brother." (Proverbs 18:24) If we have done *wrong* in the past, and the old terrible memory comes back to depress us and put us down, we can and must know the Lord Jesus as our great *High Priest*. (Hebrews 5:1-5; 7:24-25) When we are confused and lost, we must know Him as a *Leader* and *Good Shepherd*. (John 10:3, 4, 14, 15) When we feel tired and dry, He can show us Himself as our *Living Water*. In this way, we can use all temptation to bring us beautiful times with Him in our pain and trial. These times with Him will put a curtain of new and happy thoughts over our old ones. They will make it hard for us to dig back into the old clay of our bad past.

Becoming a child of God is like learning to drive on the other side of the road. When you come to Jesus, you really *do* "change sides." No real Christian stays on the same side of the road he used to live on. He now lives for Jesus. A change has happened. But for a while he must be careful. He has brought to his new life some memories of the way he used to live. He cannot afford to do things by habit. He must be careful until he has learned the new way to live and begins to do things GOD'S way by habit.

(C) Finally, temptation can come from the *Devil*. He attacks us with temptation if he thinks we are still weak enough to give in in some areas; and he saves his attacks until we are either very excited and thrilled, or very depressed and down. So watch out for either time. Be careful when marvelous things happen; be careful when everything is rotten and lonely and empty. That is when you can expect Satanic temptation.

DEALING WITH DEPRESSION

Sometimes we can really get down. And being down is dangerous. It is here that the majority of our most powerful temptations come; it is here that we most easily fall into sin. What will you do when you get down? Follow these principles to pull you out for God:

(1) First, don't *think about or struggle* with sin. There is something strange about sin; the more we *think* about it, and wrestle with it, the *bigger it grows* in our mind. Of course, that doesn't mean that we should not have victory over it! One guy said, "I never have a struggle with sin. I just *give in.*" There is a way of deliverance. But first, don't fall into the trap of constantly checking your motives and worrying about whether you are being pure or whether you are actually doing what God asks. Even *praying* over sin for too long a period may fool you into further bondage. Sin is deceitful. (Hebrews 3:12-13) Jesus never said that our path of victory is to wrestle with sin with our own strength. If something is bothering you or you are depressed, you can ask the Holy Spirit to show you if you have done, or are doing, something wrong. If you get a specific answer NAMING it, proceed with the next three steps. But if you just get a *general* feeling of wrongness, then it is probably just the Devil trying to hassle you. We will show you how to deal with him next!

(2) If the Holy Spirit has showed you something wrong, take it IMMEDIATELY to Jesus. Ask Him to *forgive* you for it and prove to Him you really are sorry by taking whatever steps you need to make it right. The same applies to temptation to sin. Don't *think too long* on what you used to do, especially if you have failed before. If you dig back into your mind and think too long on what you did wrong before, you will probably give in and do it again. This will only make your bad habits stronger. This is not the way to deal with sin or temptation. The best way is to say a firm,

"No!" and turn your mind RIGHT THEN to Jesus for help. Sin can only be beaten by faith in Jesus. We can only win over the world by faith in Him and His help. Confess your sin, ask God's forgiveness and cleansing after repentance, and then thank and trust Him for it.

(3) If you are *depressed* and don't know how to handle it, and you think it may be just the Devil, do these things: First, ask Jesus for help. The Bible says, "Submit yourself to God" (James 4:7), and that comes BEFORE resisting the Devil. Then you RESIST him in the Name of the Lord. Do it FIRMLY, and in FAITH that God will honor your obedience to His Word. Say, "Jesus — you said 'Submit yourself to the Lord.' I submit myself to you right now. You are my Lord and Master. I have done what your Word says to do. Then you said, 'Resist the Devil and he will flee from you.'" Then you should say, "Satan . . . I *resist you* in the Name of Jesus. I didn't say that — Jesus said it."

(4) Learn to use the *weapon of PRAISE*. Grab a songbook or chorus book, and sing your head off for Jesus! It doesn't matter how you sound, as long as it makes you happy, it will make God happy (Philippians 4:4). Praise scares the Devil because you are supposed to be depressed, and you are singing instead. That is unnerving to Hell. And lastly, PRAY — but NOT for yourself. That is just what the Devil wants you to do when you get depressed — pray for yourself, and turn deeper into yourself. No — pray for *others*. And Satan will very rapidly take off the pressure.

V

THE DRESSING ROOM:
Appearance

Take a look in this room. See that face in the mirror? Believe it or not — that's YOU! Now let's be honest. You're not all that you could be, and neither is anyone else. But you can and must make the most of your best points and work to improve the others.

People are not drawn to Jesus by a dull, shabby front. You are a child of the King of Kings! God *made* you, saved you! You can use what you have to bring Him glory. What you look like on the *outside* is not as important to Him as your *inside* life, yet your features, coloring, height, and figure can all contribute something to His purposes for you. Let's start with who you are. Your Father is the Lord of the Universe. Hold your head high! You are a special subject of His love and care. So what if you are different in any of the ways man says are not "in"? So what if you don't look in their eyes as "far out" as your brother, or have the talents of the girl next door? None of these things matter because you are who you are! You are important to Him.

DRESS — "MAN MAKETH THE CLOTHES "

Let's start with dress — what you choose to wear. No one can set a pattern of clothes that meet a "Christian" standard. What may be acceptable for one reason in one land may be totally unacceptable in another for a different reason. What Christians wore a hundred years ago would tab you as a "weirdo" in today's culture.  But dress *is* very important. It is an outward sign of our inward choices and life-styles. It gives an outward clue to the kind of life we like to live and the kind of person we are.

When Jesus spoke about John the Baptist, He asked the people what *they* expected to see in him: "But what did you go out to see? A man clothed in soft, expensive clothes? Those who are dressed in style and luxury live in palaces." (Luke 7:25) John the Baptist did not wear clothes acceptable with popular culture; he wore a camel-hair coat which was not bought from the local Jerusalem men's fashion counter! But the point is this: *What he wore was part of his message.* What YOU WEAR is part of YOUR message. You *say* something to people by the way you dress. It is one of the first sermons anyone hears when they first meet you. Now, what does *your* sermon say? Does it give the right kind of invitation? Does it draw attention to Jesus? Does it uplift His Name?

When man sinned, he made for himself his first set of clothes. They were "fig-leaf fashion" and weren't really the best for the cold night of judgment that was about to fall on the first sinning pair. God stepped in and clothed them properly. God's first step when He faced them with their sin was to clothe them *His* way. The people who have "overcome by the Blood of the Lamb" in the book of Revelation are marked with clothes that are white; their dress is part of their testimony. (Revelation 3:4-5) The distinguishing marks of BABYLON, the "mother of harlots," were her CLOTHES and jewelry; what she looked like was an integral part of what she was inside. The Bible opens with man being clothed, and closes with similar scenes. Your dress *is* important to God. It is not just a hang-up of a previous religious formalism. Even the death of Christ was related to clothes; the soldiers cast lots for His garments. (Matthew 27:35)

The world uses dress and fashion to project its spirit and morals, its ethics and values (or lack of them). Our way of dressing tells us something of our control or influence by this world. As time draws to a close, dress will become more and more perverted. We must stand as Christians and dress in a way that will speak, as loudly as our words, what is clean and valuable and real. Every day, the way you dress will say something to the world about Jesus and you.

Now, you *never* have to dress to impress. God has already taken a great deal of trouble to set you apart as different from the crowd. Look at yourself! Your fingerprints are different. Your voiceprints and brainwave channel are different from anyone else's in the world. Even the hair on your head is not quite the same as that of your twin brother. No Christian has to put on "special clothes" to feel like a special person. You *know* you are already. You can afford to dress in a way that is clean and comfortable, without having to follow the ways of the world around you, whether it is the Madison Avenue straight world, or the subculture in rejection of it. But remember: What you *look* like will tell the world something about God. Make it count. Learn to dress in a way that honors Christ.

THE BASIC THREE: TASTE IN DRESS

(1) Be *CLEAN:* Clothes can be old, second-hand, cheap, or very ordinary; but they should never stay dirty. Keep them washed, as neat, and clean as your life-style allows.

(2) Be *SIMPLE:* Avoid complex trimmings, complicated styles. Let your dress preach the kind of Gospel Jesus said was so simple a child could understand it.

(3) Be *SENSIBLE:* "Don't follow the latest fad" just because it is "in" at the moment. Fashion-slavery is a sign of a people-pleasing, worldly heart. Christians don't belong.

GENERAL RULES FOR DRESS

(1) Dress to *commend the Gospel*. Look like a Christian.

(2) Dress for what *you're doing*. Don't waste God's money on useless extras.

(3) Dress to *suit* your personality. Ask God to help you choose your clothes.

(4) *Never look sexually suggestive.* (Burn your old clothes if they are.)

(5) Never look *cheap*. God's beauty is an inner mark, that can't be bought in a store.

Thank God for some of the values that were restored by the counter-culture. Young people began to dress in a way that was comfortable and convenient. The new consciousness brought a deliverance from gaudy, foolish ways of living and dressing. It marked a return to plain, simple clothes with colors of earth and sky and trees. Women began to dress again in beautiful, feminine ways, instead of parading their dress as a focus for sexual consciousness. The picture may change again. The Bible only gives us guidelines in dress; it does not tell us *what* to wear, but it does tell us how to wear it.

(1) *DRESS TO DISPLAY JESUS* in your life: "The adornment of a Christian woman is not a matter of elaborate hair-styles, expensive clothes or costly jewelry, but the living of a good life." (I Timothy 2:9) The Greek word used for dress here is from a word that also means "to appease,

put down." Dress should not stir up attention to your *body;* it should only set you off *as a person* in the sight of others. Dress modestly for Jesus.

(2) *DRESS TO DRAMATIZE THE INNER YOU:* "Extremes in dress are signs of a lonely, self-centered heart. "Moreover," Jehovah said, "Because the daughters of Zion are haughty, and walk with outstretched necks and wanton eyes, walking and mincing as they go, and make a tinkling with their feet; in that day the Lord will take away the pendants and the bracelets . . . the headbands and the ankle chains . . ." (Isaiah 3:16-24) The Bible links *pride* with the way we can dress. Avoid dressing such that people notice you because you look too gaudy or too dull. No one should notice a Christian's clothes before his face.

(3) *DRESS TO PLEASE JESUS:* "And I, John, saw the holy city, new Jerusalem (God's people) coming down from God out of heaven, prepared as a bride adorned for her husband." (Revelation 21:2) "Don't be concerned about the outward beauty that depends on jewelry, or beautiful clothes, or hairstyles. Be beautiful inside, in your hearts, with the lasting charm of a gentle and quiet spirit which is so precious to God." (I Peter 3:3-4) Dress each day in the kind of clothes you would be happy to wear in heaven, if you were going "home" that day. As you look in the mirror, ask yourself, "Will *Jesus* be happy about what I'm wearing?"

CHOOSING CLOTHES — GIRLS

Here are a few guidelines to help you pick the right kind of clothes for you, if you are not average height or weight; they will help you make the most of your best points and not draw attention to your bad ones:

COLORS

If you are SHORT:
Choose clothes with *vertical* patterns, THIN motifs and fabrics. Use thin belts, straight-lined or accordian-pleated skirts. THINK tall! You are big in *God's* eyes. Don't feel funny because you are little. It is an advantage because most Christian guys like to feel protective and strong, and your size can help them feel like that when they are with you. But stay away from horizontal stripes, wide accessories that will shrink you further.

If you are TALL:
Pick out dresses with *horizontal* lines, large-patterned prints, bulkier fabrics. Buy longer jackets on separates, use wide belts, slightly-flared or soft-pleated skirts. And if you are tall; remember that God has made guys like that too, who feel funny with normal-size girls  and absolutely ridiculous with short girls. Cultivate a gentle spirit. Learn to speak with softness, so you don't seem imperious or self-sufficient in your height.

DARK colors *conceal* and *slim*; BRIGHT colors do the opposite. Choose the weights of your clothes wisely according to the work you are doing and where you will be. MEDIUM WEIGHT clothes span more seasons. Keep your hemlines about half-an-inch shorter than your coat hemlines on normal dresses.

GIRLS: PROBLEM FIGURES

You want to look nice, but your parents weren't trying as hard as they could when they had you! Use these tips to help correct a problem figure:

NECK:	Too *short* – Use minimum-clutter lines; "V" or bateau shaped necklines.
	Too *long* – Polo-type necklines; wear collars or scarves when you can.
ARMS:	Too *plump* — Use loose sleeves, not too short; just capping shoulders; end at muscled area just above the elbow or the wrist.
	Too *thin* — Cut by your sleeve at the thickest point. No sleeveless styles.
BUST:	*Flat* — Wear bloused top, not tightly-fitting.
	Large — Fluid, unbroken lines to hips — no high-waisted tops.
WAIST:	*Long* — Disguise by Empire or low-waisted bodice.
	Short — Better over-all balance with a shaped leather belt; fits below waist on lower curved edge.
THIGHS:	Can be hidden to some extent by a flared skirt.
LEGS:	Shortness can be lengthened a bit by a slim dress with a not-too-long skirt.
FEET:	If they are a little long, shorten with higher heel; this also lengthens ankle-to-knee.
HANDS:	*Large* — Use a glove for special occasions 3-4" above wrist. Beige preferable to white.
	Small — Don't wear chunky rings, watches, etc.

ACCESSORIES

At least one set in a basic color: Black, brown, white, navy, or gray. A beige dark enough for winter, light enough for summer is the best compromise. If you want an extra set, get them in a brighter set of colors but be sure the shades match each other.

SHOES:	*Heavier* — Use a stockier heel. No tight, thin shoe-straps!
	Taller — More medium heels. You don't need to wear flats all the time.

HANDBAGS: Spend as much as you can afford to get a strong and good looking one. A good bag dresses the plainest outfits, lasts for years with a shape that doesn't date. Stay away from over-stuffed or over-large bags; they are not suitcases.

ABOVE ALL: Dress modestly. Don't dress sensually. Dress like a woman, but dress like the princess of the Royal Family you are. Preserve your unique femininity. Don't try to copy maleness; stay away from rugged, tweedy or chunky fabrics. Keep your dresses delicate, swishy, and female. God made you a woman; be proud of it.

HAIR: GIRLS

Shampoo and wash once a week. Brush it well; "fifty strokes" for cleanliness and shine! Wear it trimmed and tidy. No loose straggly bits; it can have that billowy "wind-blown" look guys love, but not the *bedraggled* one. Stay away from elaborate styles; they are a waste of God's money, and don't last. Your hair is your glory. The Bible says it is a covering and a protection for you, an outward sign of spiritual understanding that you are protected by your Christian brothers who love Christ. If you can wear it *long*, do so; it makes you all the girl God calls you to be and adds a crown of beauty to you. "...If a woman has long hair it is a glory to her; for her hair is given her for a covering."

HAIR SHADE:	Silver Blond	Golden Blond	Brunette
CLOTHES COLOR:			
"Feminine" *BLUE*	Any shade, except electric ones.	As before for silver	Brilliant delphinium, cobalt, sky-blue, navy, and royal blues with paler skins.
"Confident" *RED*	Less brilliant reds; rosy-reds, look good.	No overpowering reds; warm Chestnut shades better.	Any red terrific, specially scarlet and flame.
"Eye-Catching" *YELLOW*	Most yellow ochres and ambers.	"Golden girl" look as before.	Devonshire cream good, beware of deeper yellows.
"Basic" *BLACK*	Look more fair and fragile.	As Before.	Dramatic, but cool.
"Show-off" *WHITE*	Stark white can look frosty with paler skins.	Stark white best.	Pale skins look ethereal; darker tans contrast stunningly.
"Variable" *GREEN*	Silvery sage-greens best for you.	Yellow-greens look best on you.	Brilliant chartreuse, lime, emerald; paler skins: Peppermint colors and shades

HAIR SHADE:	Mid-Brown	Red-heads
CLOTHES COLOR:		
"Feminine" *BLUE*	Sunny, bright blues; turquoise, Prussian and blue-greens.	Navy a brilliant foil for you.
"Confident" *RED*	Soft corals, raspberry tones; sharp shades can drown you out.	Gingery, tawny reds, not blue reds. Dark copper wine or clear reds look superb.
"Eye-Catching" *YELLOW*	Rich gold, burnt yellows, warm gold tans, acid yellows are too hard.	Magic in yellow with muted, autumn tones pick up your own color.
"Basic" *BLACK*	Add some color in accessories.	Black can make you glow like fire; White skins look whiter.
"Show-off" *WHITE*	Creamy-whites best; icy-whites can wash you out.	High-color: creamy tones; for creamy skins, milk-white best.
"Variable" *GREEN*	Look fairer in green; for mousier complexion, try almond, sage, pine green shades.	Emeralds so obvious; try off-beat shades like bottle-green, dark moss.

NOTES: Use this chart to help you pick clothes that match your kind of hair-coloring and skin-coloring. The color of the clothes you pick will determine the kind of effect you create by the message of your dress. This will serve as a rough guide to help you choose wisely in a way that will best compliment what God has given you in the way of natural looks.

RED, YELLOW, or *WHITE* are not usually good for the timid, shy, or plump person: *RED* "heats up" high color complexions. Soft, pale *BLUES* can look too "pretty-pretty" with bows or frills. *BLACK* emphasizes YOU, so groom carefully when you wear this color. No hard crimson or too-pastel shades. For "camouflage" colors, try *BEIGE* or *GRAYS.* Anyone can wear these colors, but they do nothing for you — too much will make you "fade away." Add accessory colors to make them live; choose ones that will "play up" your own complexion.

VI

THE WORKSHOP: Abilities

A busy room this, especially in your spare time. It's the *workshop*, where all the jobs that need to get done are finished. What gifts do *you* have? What talents has God given you? Are they all surrendered to His service? Are they all being used for His glory? God has a job for you to do in this "century 21." *You* are a vitally important part of the Christian task force! Let's take a good look at you and help you to discover your talents and abilities.

> "What we *are* is God's gift to us.
> What we *become* is our gift to God."

Most of us have felt that awful feeling of "not fitting in" anywhere. This is part of growing up, and a *scary* part at that! Now — let's find out what you can do!

(1) *Get a PAPER AND PENCIL.* Head up one side of your sheet *"Abilities"* and

the other side *"Goals."* Be honest! (And none of that phony "I can't do anything" routine.)

(2) On the side marked *"Abilities,"* write down everything you feel you *can* do. THINK! You don't have to *excel* in them; just if you enjoy doing it or have done it before. Cover all fields: physical, mental, social, spiritual. Can you play a sport well? Any favorite subject at school? A gift in speaking, singing, acting? A writing talent? Are you mechanically, electrically or chemically minded? Get along well with people?

(3) Now *CLASSIFY* them according to how well you can do them — terrific, very good, okay, fair, passable, p.w.a.p. (pass with a push). Don't exaggerate or underestimate.

(4) Read through the list again and add any others that may come to mind. Take a good look at the finished paper. It may be very full, or like the average person, just medium. You may be surprised to find out just how much you can really do! Add, if you like, any *"Assets"* — things that you have naturally that can help in any field (even in things you have never done) like good health, keen mind, likeable personality, etc.

THIS IS A PICTURE OF THE REAL YOU. Someone once said we are *three* people every day; the person people *think* us to be, the person *we* want people to think we are, and the person we *actually* are. This will help you see just what you have and are. Be honest.

(5) Now, on the second side headed "Goals," put down what you REALLY WANT TO BE. Be specific. Don't just put "a better person" or something vague. Ask the Lord to give you some help here, as you will want all your goals for His glory.

(6) Be *REALISTIC*. Don't just put down "a movie star" or "a millionaire" if that is some vague, romantic dream that you don't really want to work towards, but just wish sometimes you could feel what it was like. If God has given you a clue to what He wants you to do, this should be your main goal. If not, write down the things you would really enjoy doing (especially later in life), if you could really do what you wanted to.

(7) Now *COMPARE* your sheets. Are any of your "abilities" possible steps to one of your "goals"? These are the ones you will be able to develop effectively in God's pattern for your life, as they are all talents He has developed in your personality. EACH of us has a specific place in His purpose which NO ONE else in the world can fill. There is something waiting for you in the world that only *you* can do.

CHECK your goals carefully. CROSS OFF any that have selfish motives behind them. God cannot help you obtain these. If you are unsure, right now commit them to Him, and ask Him to control them. He can take them out of the way if they will harm your spiritual life in any way. That's your "LIFE INVENTORY." Armed with a better look at who you are and what you want to do, let's get on to the —

SUCCESS PLAN FOR CHRISTIANS

If you follow this plan for developing your ability, you will find you *cannot fail* to achieve what you feel God will let you do! It will be *impossible* to fail, for God will open doors and work miracles for you to help you do what others may think cannot be done. But you must really *work* at it and do all that God asks you to do.

(1) Choose *ONE* thing at a time. Too many goals ruin your concentration. Pick the one thing you REALLY want most!

(2) Take a card and write on one side of it your goal. On the *other* side, write down these two Scripture verses: "Ask and it shall be given you; seek and you SHALL find; knock

and it SHALL be opened to you." (Matthew 7:7) And, "With God, NOTHING shall be impossible." (Luke 1:37) Now, take this goal to God. Tell Him why you want to see it happen. Be perfectly honest with Him. Show Him these two promises. Tell Him, "Father, this is what is on my heart to make me a better person for You. Here are two promises You made. I claim them in faith to help me fulfill this for Your glory."

(3) Now, *stop thinking* about possible hindrances. That is God's job to fix, not yours. Don't be afraid that you won't be able to do it! If it is for the Lord's glory, you MUST SUCCEED. You CANNOT FAIL if God is in it.

(4) THINK CONSTANTLY of your goal. Picture yourself as having *already achieved* your goal. Carry around your card with you and look at it morning and night. We begin to BECOME WHAT WE THINK ABOUT — your thoughts mold your life. That is why it is important that God controls your aims. See yourself as doing what you have always wanted to do.

(5) Give yourself a *30-day test*. For a FULL THIRTY DAYS, you must follow your goal, EVERY DAY. Persistence is your faith in action. During that time, do MORE than you have to. Give of yourself more, and don't let petty things sidetrack or worry you. Recommit your goal to God every morning and night. If you fail to follow the plan the full time, you must BEGIN AGAIN and go ANOTHER 30 DAYS. Go *out of your way* to help others. Work STEADILY towards your goal. It won't be easy, but give it your best.
REMEMBER — if you fail, you must BEGIN AGAIN.

(6) If MONEY enters your goal, then *give* at least 10% to God and *SAVE* at least 10%. Think of your money and time,

talents and opportunities as possession ON LOAN from the Lord. GIVING to some need that He lays on your heart is only INVESTING His property in some valuable concern. If you are a conscientious steward of His goods, He will repay all money invested under His guidance multiplied times. You can't outgive Him.

(7) REMEMBER: You and God are always a MAJORITY. He cannot fail — and with Him on your side, *you* CANNOT either! Thank Him every day, when it gets rough, as well as when things go well. Keep a calm, happy, and trusting spirit. Be like a child looking with joy and excitement to another new day. HE IS ABLE!

HOW TO FIT MORE INTO A DAY

Part of the problem of not successfully using your abilities is what seems to be another problem: not having enough time during a day. Here are some hints to help you get more into your day.

(1) *Plan a SCHEDULE for yourself.* You may have never done this before. Try it now. Some men who really changed the world for God found time because of their solid self-discipline. *John Wesley* said in the 24 hours of a day that he had eight hours to sleep, eight hours to work, eat, and study, and the other eight hours he could give to God. *Jonathan Edwards* disciplined his life so that he often had 13 hours a day to spend in study! Self-discipline is one of the parts of the fruit of the Spirit. Here's help for you:

Pick a time when you *have* to get up. Set it according to your responsibilities. Then set another time when you *ought* to get to bed. You can find out how much sleep you need by going to sleep in a perfectly dark room for a week and averaging out the time it takes for you to wake up naturally, by yourself, without an alarm. Most people need between 7-8 hours, some a little longer or shorter. Set your "night limit" by this time.

Now *plan out* your day. If you have a job or school, you know how long it takes to do it each day, what time you will have to leave to get there, what time you can expect to be home. This gives you your second big division in time. Leave that until later.

Take the first "block" of time, that between waking up and leaving for work or school. How *many* hours do you have here? Now write down, in order, the things you usually do after you get up — make your bed, wash, dress, eat breakfast, etc. Write them out and beside each one put the SHORTEST TIME you can do each job *properly* in. *Time yourself* next to see just how long it has taken you to do these things. Now, go into the rest of your day in the same way. Divide it into big blocks and then subdivide each block up with rough times for each small part of the day. It may help you to put things in a "MUST DO," "SHOULD DO," or "COULD DO," category. This will help you to put priority on the things that *have* to be done and the good things that *might* be done, if you have time. You can use this same idea, by the way, to *make a list of the night before* if you have a whole lot of things on your mind to do the following day, and you're worried about them. It will help clear your mind and give you a "priority list" to tack in order of importance.

(2) Now, the fun begins. You should have a "rough" time for each thing you have to do in your day. Tomorrow when you get up, spend each small section *having a race* with yourself. Compete with your own time. *How long* does it take you to make the bed? Today you will see if you can do it just as well with a *minute* knocked off the time. How long did it take you to wash and shave or get your face ready for the day? You will do it faster today. Race yourself! If you have a five-minute timer like an egg timer or kitchen timer, you can use that to "race against the clock." Do it in fun, but work as fast as you can. Pace yourself *against* yourself. Win from each day a minute here, a couple of minutes there. See

just how much time you have won before your next fixed responsibility time arrives!

(3) Use the *"nothing"* times to do something! Often during a day we have times when we are inactive: Waiting in line for a bus or train, traveling to and from work, waiting for a kettle to boil, a bath to run, someone to come home. How many hours can be used of these "nothing" times! Read a helpful book, do a little study; or if you have nothing else to do, spend some few moments in prayer or in quiet meditation on the goodness of God. Make it a practice to carry your Bible with you everywhere you go. When you wait for someone or are doing nothing of profit, break it open and read until your time is up.

(4) *Learn to SELECT.* You can't read *all* books, so make sure the ones you *do* read are ones directly related to your goals. You can't go to all meetings, so go only to those that will best help forward what God is doing in your life. SELECT. The good is the enemy of the BEST. Learn to reject things that you could do which would take time away from the more important things.

(5) *Do the HARD THINGS FIRST. Make* yourself do them. Don't get into the bad habit of putting off the worst things until the last. Tackle them early when you are fresh. Begin all the worst tasks first and get them out of the way as soon as you can. This is one secret of discipline. It will help make you a man or woman who can really make the most of you time. Tackle the hard jobs first and finish with the easiest ones.

(6) *Learn to be PUNCTU-AL.* Stick to your schedules. If you have an appointment get there on time. It is a bad testimony and poor stewardship of God's time to arrive late everywhere. It will help if you keep a diary of appointments. Consult it often, plan ahead,

leave plenty of time to get there, and don't leave things until the last minute. If it helps, set your watch forward five to ten minutes; sometimes it helps to get you there earlier, especially if you forget it *was* set forward!

(7) Finally, *AVOID ALL SIDETRACKS*. There are many fun things you could do, but you are a child of God, and are in training for the King of All Kings' family. Avoid all petty interferences with God's goal for your life; don't fret, worry or brood over others' interference with this; leave it in His hands. Keep resolutely at what you are doing. Take the chance to discipline any area where you are wasting too much time, money, or energy; carefully think through things like eating, dress, "relaxation," or entertainment. Get to bed before you get overly tired; give the next new day to God and rest the one that has just passed in His loving and understanding hands.

VII

THE BATHROOM: Cleanliness

BODY — CARE OF THE TEMPLE

PERSONAL CLEANLINESS: A DAILY shower or bath with soap — ears, neck, face, feet, and fingernails included! Only ten minutes a day, but there is truth in that old saying "Cleanliness is next to Godliness."

TEETH: "Brush your teeth after every meal and see your dentist twice a year." If you have bad breath, don't breathe it to a soul! Slip a mint into your mouth now and then. Or carry a breath spray or drops with you; use especially before counseling people.

DEODORANT: Essential to have around. Perspiration does cause odor that can spoil your witness. Don't try to use this in place of a wash or shower; it is an "extra guard."

Girls: A perfumed soap, light skin fragrance, or bath water, with a personalized, scenty powder makes you nice to be with. Again, use "as well as" not "instead."

Guys: There are special lines for men, but avoid any of the lines that push you towards a femininity that will dishonor God and dilute your maleness. A good after-shave can wake you up and make you feel great; don't "wash" in it; just pat it on.

FEET: They carry you everywhere; and God says that your feet, as a Christian, are blessed! "How beautiful upon the mountains are the feet of him that brings good tidings, that published peace; that brings good tidings of good, that published salvation; that says to Zion, 'Your God reigns!' "(Isaiah 52:7) Your feet get the most work; but how often do you honor them? WASH them every day. It was a thing they did in Jesus' day. (John 13:5) DRY them carefully; if you forget, you could get skin trouble like "athlete's foot." A good antiseptic and deodorant foot powder for shoes and socks is a help.

NAILS: CARE and CLIPPING! Fingernails should be shaped and kept trimmed to a moderate length. Toenails must be cut ACROSS THE TOP, not down the sides, or you may have ingrown toenail trouble. Keep them CLEAN — a little nail file or knife with a similar gadget on it will fit handily into your pocket. Don't go fixing your nails in public!

SKIN: Teenage years are often marked by oiliness of skin and distressing outbreaks of pimples. Correct diet and extra-soapy washes will usually correct things after a while. There are medical preparations you can buy to help dry up blemishes.

VOICE: Heard yourself on a tape recorder? It can be shattering! Do you sound shrill, unsure, bored, cold, impatient, or "mousey" with a breathless squeak? All flaws can be improved or corrected with a little help. Determine to control your speech. Don't slur or rush words; practice speaking slowly, distinctly, and clearly. LISTEN to your REAL VOICE. If you don't have a tape recorder, speak in a corner with your face to the walls, hands cupped behind your ears with palms facing the walls. That's what you sound like! Correct the faults you notice. Watch words like "Yeah;

goin' " etc. Don't leave out endings! SMILE as you talk over a telephone. It puts life into your voice.

MANNERS are just as important. Say "Thank-you," and write notes for the same. Be just as courteous at home as you are with special friends. If you are complimented say "Thank-you," not "Oh, this old thing!" Be natural, relax, and enjoy other people. And learn to WALK TALL. Imagine your head is held up with a star. Carry yourself as God's child.

Part of your daily appearance is personal discipline of your life. A disciple is a DISCIPLINED ONE. Nothing good ever comes by shortcuts, avoiding tough challenges, or by easy, soft living. Your growing body needs development, so here's a —

PHYSICAL FITNESS PROGRAM:

The Double-Five Program: You need only five minutes a day for these five exercises to help get you slim and trim for the work of Jesus:

(1) *BEND-DOWNS:* Feet astride, arms upward. Bend forwards to the floor, touching with fingertips. Then stretch upwards and backwards. Do not strain to keep knees straight. Exercise for thirty seconds, rest ten, and repeat for the last twenty seconds.

(2) *TWIST-AROUNDS:* Feet astride, arms upward. Touch floor outside right foot, then between feet, then outside left foot, then circle-bend backwards as far as possible with arms above head. Reverse directions for another twenty seconds. Exercise 30, rest 10, repeat 20.

(3) *SIT-UPS:* Lie on back, feet together, legs straight, arms straight overhead. Sit up and touch the toes, keeping

arms and legs straight. If necessary, use a chair and hook feet under. (Don't use a light one or you'll turn it over on you!) Exercise 30, rest 10, repeat 20.

(4) *PUSH UPS:* Lie on front, palms flat on floor. Straighten arms to lift body. Chest must touch the floor each time. Exercise for thirty seconds, rest ten, repeat twenty.

(5) *RUN AROUNDS:* Run in one place for three, ten-second intervals, with a ten second rest period between each one. Knees should be raised to waist level or higher. A brisk trot or run could be substituted for this.

BUILDING MUSCLE AND TONE

Use "isometrics" to help you develop athletically. Contraction of key muscles can be effective in strengthening and developing them. It works very simply; just TENSE the part of the body you want to develop. Easy? Yes! Your muscles "work" against each other, mutually developing them. For an overall build up, stand in a doorway about as high as your extended arms, or lie between two walls with your feet flat on one wall and your palms flat on the other. Now PUSH — "tensing" your muscles all over. Hold it for a FULL TEN SECONDS — if done properly, your body should "quiver" with the strain. CONTINUE this for only TEN seconds every day; and in a month or two, you will see a difference! To develop any other part, use the same principle. Arms, feet — push or pull against a fixed bar. The SUPPORT must be IMMOVABLE or nearly so, and you should apply the contraction PERPENDICULARLY to it. If you like, use a friend to apply resistance. Sometimes you will not even need a support; isometrics can function wherever you can tense muscles properly.

TAKING CARE OF YOUR BODY

"Your body is the temple of the Holy Spirit." (I Corinthians 6:19) Proper care is essential for good health and a radiant witness. Check these:

(1) DIET: THREE balanced meals a day, especially if you have to do physical work early. Start with breakfast; or if you are in lighter work, eat a good lunch and later supper. We have to get certain kinds of food daily for present health and energy and to help prevent sickness and dental troubles.

OVERWEIGHT? Not caused so much by eating a LOT, but by eating the WRONG THINGS. (Too many sweets or candy, cakes, soft drinks or pop—ugh!) If you have real weight problems, and it is not glandular (a medical problem), try a fast. (See: "Something To Try" - page 81).

UNDERWEIGHT? Again, wrong things. Your diet should have protein foods: Meat, eggs, milk, cheese. You have a problem that is more fun to correct than the previous one.

A correct diet can do much to change your appearance either way. Your meals should include VEGETABLES (yellow and green, cooked and raw), FRUITS (one citrus, like oranges, one other), MILK (at least three glasses - one at each meal), WHOLE GRAIN cereal or bread, MEAT or POULTRY, FISH and EGGS.

(2) *SLEEP:* Not less than 7-8 hours a night for teenagers. It will differ a little from person to person; but what a difference that extra hour makes to your looks and vitality! Don't SLEEP TOO LONG — that can make you just as sluggish as too little sleep. The Bible says two things about your sleep: (1) "He gives His beloved sleep." (Psalms 127:2); "If we walk wisely with God, and listen to His counsel, our sleep shall be sweet." (Proverbs 3:24); and (2) too much sleep can make our lives poor and unproductive: "How long will you sleep, O sluggard? When will you wake up from your slum-

ber? A little sleep, a little slumber, a little folding of the hands to sleep; so shall your poverty come as a robber, and want as an armed man." (Proverbs 6:9-11)

(3) *EXERCISE:* As well as your physical fitness program, get involved in a sport of some kind. Every Christian should be active in some sport. It will help your physical development, keep you fit, and give you valuable contacts for the Lord. When you find one you like, WORK AT IT! Play for ALL and PLAY TO WIN. Sports teach sportsmanship and Christian leadership. The Apostle Paul often uses sports illustrations to describe the Christian life. In I Corinthians 9:24-27 he says, "You know that only one person gets a prize for being in a race even if many people run. You must run so that you will win the prize. Everyone who runs does many things so that his body will be strong. In the same way, I run straight for the place at the end of the race. I fight to win. I do not box the air. I keep working over my body. I make it obey me." The Lord wants us to have strong, disciplined bodies. Jesus, Himself, was a carpenter, who in Bible days had to be both strong and skilled. The Bible tells us that, "He grew strong in mind and body." (Luke 2:52) We are to love God with all our strength. (Mark 12:30) If we use sports to do this and can serve Jesus with a better body because of our sports, God is gladdened.

Jesus can help you play well. The trials and pressures of sport will give you a chance to learn patience and forgiveness. You can earn respect both on and off the field or court by being tough in body and strong in faith. Team sports can teach you to get along with others and carry your share of the load. And many, many chances to witness to others can and will come in your sports time. When you go out to play, go out for God! *When you play, play for Jesus!* Make each shot count for Him, put out your best because you are playing to the grandstand of Heaven. And you will play the best games of your life because you will play for His glory. He will be watching you! You will play to win.

SOMETHING TO TRY — FASTING

Before any big, important event in your life, when you really need to do your best with God's help, there is a Christian secret you might like to try. For an important speech, prayer, message, or game: FASTING may be a real help. It is an indication that you are EARNEST, that there is something you want so greatly, you will put everything aside to get it. It's honestly, sincerely — sometimes desperately — reaching out for God and His will. We put Him first, above food, water, friends.

FASTING for the Christian is simply the voluntary missing of a life need. It is not always food — it can be rest, sleep, friends, or drink. But used in the Bible it usually means not eating food for a certain time. It can help you in two ways: it can rest and clean your body by not weighing it down with food; it can draw your heart close to God since you are spending the same time you would usually give to eating in prayer instead. You can fast from anything that you are willing to temporarily sacrifice for God.

It must be VOLUNTARY, something you choose to do yourself. There is no value in doing it because you are told to. God will not force you to fast, but if you really need that extra intensity, it is there to help.

It must be PRIVATE. If you tell anyone you are fasting, so they will be convinced of your spirituality, God will not bless you for it. Fasting must be done for HIM. If you go around boasting about it to others, you already have your reward. Of course, you may have to tell parents, or friends who know your eating habits, so as not to worry them; but this is different. When you fast, don't go around looking haggard, dead-on-your-feet, and wiped-out. That is not fulfilling the fasting conditions laid down in Matthew 6:16-18.

It must be SENSIBLE. You won't want to fast for weeks as a teenager, nor if you have a demanding or strenuous job to do as well. Holiday or weekends are best; you will be able to control your activity better. If you want to go on a long fast, start with a few smaller ones and then work up with rests in between. Long fasts need longer rest periods both during and after the fast.

It must be THOUGHTFUL. Don't inconvenience parents or friends by being difficult! On a long fast, you must drink MUCH WATER, at least seven GLASSES A DAY. If you want a real fast, don't drink anything else; especially coffee or tea. Long fasts can last from two to three or even four weeks. The most difficult part is the first five to six days. You may feel headachy, sick to your stomach, and tired, as your body poisons are emptied out. Keep flushing your system out with water. After the worst peak is over, you can go many, many days without real appetite for food. STOP the fast if HUNGER returns; this is a sign that the body has used up all its reserves, and if you go on any longer you will begin to starve. Be *very careful* in breaking a long fast; take as LONG TO BREAK IT AS YOU DID TO TAKE IT. Use juices, clear, non-milky soups, etc., until you come gradually back to normal diet.

Use your normal action time, eating, pleasure, company time, for prayer instead. Talk to Jesus during this time. Read the Bible. You'll be richly blessed.

VII (CONT.)

GROWING UP WITH GOD — Girls

Hi, Girls:

You'll be feeling many strange and perhaps bewildering changes in your teen years. In all areas, physical, mental, social, and spiritual, there will be new happenings and problems. Life will be kind of UNPREDICTABLE — up and down! You'll change a lot.

That's why it's so important to know Christ as a teenager. You will face the same problems as others — just as tough, if not tougher — but with your hand in His, you won't face them alone.

Between the ages of roughly 13-15 you'll be *GROWING*. It will be hard for you here! You will mature faster than guys your same age. This brings its own special problems.

PHYSICAL: Your body will blossom out into young womanhood. There will be new clothes to try and buy as you develop. There will be new problems too, as you experience for the first time the special problems of becoming a woman. You'll begin to menstruate, that periodic monthly flow of blood that signals that God has given you the gift of becoming a mother. Your breasts will begin to develop, and with these sexual changes, your body will become alive to new stirrings of romance and love. This is beautiful, but you must be careful with your feelings. They are so much a part of your body at this time that they will be very easily stirred up romantically. Ride it out, little one! Protect your body from being stirred into sexual passion, just as you would not try to force a rosebud open before it has had time to become a rose. All girls feel as strange as you do during these years. Don't let these big changes hassle you.

MENTAL: Here's the time to "soak up" as much as you can. Now your mind may not be too much on studies at school. You find it hard to see any use for what you are learning here, but it's the best time to learn things. Don't fill your mind with "true romance" comics, books on love stories, and films on making-out with guys! I know how much this will clamor to take first place on your life. But live in balance, by living in Jesus' love. You will frustrate people, because you don't stay interested in one thing for very long. "Change" is the name of your game; you get really excited about one thing, but within a week it has worn off and you are on some new trip. You change boyfriends like clothes. Be careful of your emotions. They will change suddenly, sometimes without warning. Don't get disturbed by "dark" days or "rainy-day Mondays."

They get *all* girls your age down. You'll feel on top of the totem pole one day, the next, so low that you'll feel you have to reach up to touch bottom. Remember: Your body is going through some rough changes; you are un-fortunately connected with it! These feelings are NATURAL; they will level off soon.

SOCIAL: Beware! Having changing feelings, being in-curably romantic, and having a woman's body with a teenager's mind all spell "temptation" in the social area. You'll be interested in guys, but the ones your age will mostly seem like babies, thanks to your faster physical maturity. Naturally, since they seem only interested in cars, sports, and gangs, you will feel attracted to guys who are probably older than you by at least three or four years. You may fall desperately in love with your English or history teacher because he smiled at you one day. Can you see the danger? Unless your date life is really controlled by Jesus, there's danger — real danger — of giving into your rocketing romantic feelings and getting into trouble.

Young love can be wonderful fun, even though it only lasts a little while (though you dream of it lasting *forever* and can't *imagine* ever loving anyone else than the guy who JUST SAID "Hello" to you — until next week!) The pain and joy of learning to win a boy's interest and affection can teach you a lot about life. But let Jesus stay in control, always there to guard you like a Big Brother who loves you and wants to keep you from hurt. Watch your associations; guard your sexual purity; don't buy the current ideas of loose living; you have time to watch how they work out in the private Hells of those who lost the great debate, wound up disgraced, shamed, and alone.

SPIRITUAL: You'll be looking for answers — *real* answers. At this time, you will have a lot of doubts about God, the Bible, and Christian things. This is a hard time for you. You *feel* like a woman, but you may still be treated like a child. Because you will have real hassles with your feelings, you will wonder sometimes if you really are a Christian; if God really does exist; if He really can answer prayer; and if you can really be sure of spiritual things. Don't be afraid of having doubts. God doesn't mind you asking questions, as long as you are really willing to find some answers from Him. Spend a lot of

time in prayer and reading your Bible. The Devil will try to keep you away from God's Word because you will find the answers to so many of your questions there. As you learn to think for yourself and to make your own decisions, you will need His steady hand to help you through the rough places. Learn to lean on His love. He will bring you through these difficult years with happiness.

Round about 16-18, stage TWO will creep up on you overnight until one morning — Crunch! You will realize you are "sweet sixteen" and it's time to REORGANIZE YOUR LIFE.

PHYSICAL: Your body will be fully developed by now. You will have gotten used to its problems and had some time to learn to control it. These are the years for those of you who are athletic to really shine. You will find your body is so together that you can break records on court, field, or track. Go to it! Learn to use your skill and poise in physical disciplines for the glory of God.

MENTAL: Suddenly you'll be able to USE all that stuff you learned the last three or four years. Those of you girls who are more academic will really shine now; maybe you'll be your class "brain" (although of course, you'll be very modest about it and not use it to make all your boy friends feel like Charlie Brown). You will be learning more than girls your age did ten years ago; far more things than most of your parents ever knew about at this age. You will be put under pressure to worship at the shrine of education; *don't* let it become a god in your life. Let God be "Boss" of your study life. He can use your mind to take you to the top for His glory; you may be able to help other kids in your class who don't have as many answers as you do. It may lead to a chance for witness.

SOCIAL: Guys your age ARE interested in you now — VERY! These years are beautiful, and you can make many lovely, though sometimes fragile friendships. You may go through a "hard-to-get" period around now; guys will feel awkward in asking you out, and you will lose some of that giggly, "overly excited" attitude you had before and become a demure, mysterious woman. You will have a lot of dates, and that's good — you will be learning to handle friendship and affection with others. But keep close to God and no serious dates yet; keep it light and learn to mix with many different brothers and sisters.

SPIRITUAL: Most of the girls you know are probably pretty skeptical about spiritual things. You'll need a lot more answers, and you will be excited to find that the Bible does not ask "blind" faith of us. We should "study to show ourselves approved to God." He will give you some real foundations to stand on. Many of your friends who are living without Jesus will now find that the sandy grounds of human ideas which they once took refuge in are starting to sink underneath them. By now, a lot of your friends will have made some bad mistakes; but some won't have learned from them. "Anything you do is right as long as it feels good" — this will be a common idea in the crowd. This is the time to really get squared away with God; to get both your head and heart straight. The choices you make *now* will deeply affect your life and help shape your destiny under God. A solid and intelligent commitment to the Lord Jesus now may save your wholeness, your dreams, your future friendships, marriage, and ministry. Do it, and do it with your whole heart.

Finally, you make it to the last rung where you'll be making many of your final important decisions. These will be choices that will take the rest of your life to live out. From 19-24 is *EXPANSION* time. During these years you will learn to be *better* at what you have alreaded decided to do with your life.

PHYSICAL: Your body is now fully mature; you know its capacities and its capabilities. You are beginning to understand your moods and feelings in relationship to your own personal chemistry from week to week. Girls, you are women now; young adults, ready to face the shining, scary, troubled, and beautiful world around you. Congratulations! The next years to come will often be the years in which God brings to you some guy to share your life and love; between about 20-25 are the years when most girls marry, although with some it's a little later. Make it a point not to marry before you are at least in your twenties; enjoy your single womanhood, and leave your marriage in the hands of God. Don't worry if you aren't proposed to on your nineteenth birthday; and don't rule out the possibility of a creative *single* life. Although it is usually God's will for girls your age to marry, sometimes He has tasks that require a special woman with unique gifts and abilities to serve Him in a single ministry. Relax in the hands of your loving Father in heaven and know that His whole heart is set on making *you* the happiest, holiest woman He can. And if you aren't sure which calling is to be yours, stay *single* until God clearly says otherwise. It's better to be single wishing you were married, than married wishing you were single!

MENTAL: Those high school friends of yours who never came over to God's side are almost all skeptical, completely skeptical. A few of the liberal or radical may have joined any one of a dozen existing liberation or radical political groups to give them a vehicle for their hurt and their rejection of Biblical morality. You will

have decided what you are going to do; all your learning now will be centered on carrying out that goal. Make your choices wisely; guard your mind and heart from vain philosophies and humanistic ethics. In the pages of God's Word, you will find out as much about freedom, love, meaning, truth, and value as you can intelligently handle, and more.

SOCIAL: Here, in His will, God will lead you to your life-partner, God's man for your life. Sooner or later, you may have a home, begin a family. Some of your youth outreach activities for Christ will be either specialized or curtailed. These years will be those that build lifelong friendships, years that will cement lasting relationships.

SPIRITUAL: Many of your unsaved friends will be hard, bitter, and disillusioned by life's apparent emptiness. Some will have been used by the men to whom they gave themselves, hoping for some taste of real love and affection; they may be deeply bitter, and may conceal their hatred for men by flattery or even prostitution. Some will have become pregnant, given up their babies, or aborted them; others will have felt pushed into marriages they had to go through with because they got so far in they couldn't back out. But God is in the work of reshaping the hardest lives. When a woman gets hurt, she hurts more deeply than most men of her age and her experiences. It can make her very hard. But the same Lord Jesus Who spoke to the woman at the well can speak to women today and restore joy and liberation to their hearts and lives. You must be available. You be a friend who is ready and sympathetic, quick to show compassion and care. God can use you and wants to do so. There is such a needy world around you. Ahead of you lies your whole future and, with that future, part of Earth's destiny. Walk with love and faith into it, and know that Jesus has gone before you to make the rough places smooth before your feet.

Growing up with God can give you years which you can look back to with thankfulness and joy. Have many memories of lovely things and beautiful happenings you can carry with you into the future with Jesus! Don't be afraid to WHOLLY TRUST Him. Give yourself to Him with the same commitment and devotion a girl would give the man she chooses to be her husband, lover, and the father of her children. Let the whole world know that you belong to Him; body, soul, and spirit. Without Him, life is not worth living.

Be a WOMAN of God — in the way you look, dress, act, speak, and live. Be a real "I Timothy 4:12" person. And girls — God bless you, the WORLD is yours, for you and God to share — TOGETHER.

VII (CONT.)

GROWING UP WITH GOD — Guys

Hi, Fellows:

You'll be facing many strange and perhaps bewildering changes in your teen years. In all four areas; mental, physical, social, and spiritual, there will be new happenings and problems. Life will be kind of UNPREDICTABLE — up and down! You'll change a lot. Life will seem to be filled with all kinds of hassles and pressures.

That's why it's so important to know Christ as a teenager. You will face the same problems as others — just as tough, if not tougher — but with your life under His command, you won't face them *alone*. Jesus will be there to care, to help, to understand.

Between the ages of roughly 13-15, you'll be *GROWING*. It may be embarrassing! You'll perhaps feel and act awkward. You'll bug a lot of people. But cheer up — you'll survive!

PHYSICAL: During these "grow" years, you will do just that — grow! Your arms and legs will shoot out like bean poles; and you'll drive your parents nuts trying to keep you in clothes that fit for more than a few months, as you outsprout everything. You will sometimes feel funny because you will *look* funny. Your body will grow out, but it won't have any real muscle or great strength yet. It will be hard to control, and things won't always go quite the way you want them to. Because you are learning to get it all together in your body, you will probably be clumsy: Breaking dishes, tripping over things, bashing into any object that is slightly smaller than a medium-sized elephant. Your parents may encourage you in these experiments with co-ordination by such words as, "You clumsy clod!" or, "What have you busted now?" All of which will help you feel a bigger idiot than you actually are. Your VOICE will bother you to no end because suddenly it will freak-out on you. Once you had a nice soprano squeak; one day, right in the middle of talking to someone you want to impress, it will suddenly self-destruct into a low growl. But it's all a natural part of growing up. Don't let it bug you too much.

MENTAL: Here's the time to "soak up" as much as you can. Now, your mind may be not exactly rapt about your studies in school. You will often find it hard to see any use for what you are learning here, but it is the *best* time to study. Take my word for it; what you store in your head now will suddenly make you feel like a genius in just a few more years. Now you will frustrate all kinds of people at home, at church, and at school because you don't stay interested in any one thing for long. You'll be turned on to a lot of different things — cars, hobbies, secret gangs, judo, and stamp-collecting — then, just like that, lose interest. *Change* is the name of your game; you get really excited about one thing, and then within a couple of weeks it has worn off and you try something else. This is frustrating for your parents and your youth pastor, but it's good for you. You are learning an interest in a lot of things; some of your interests will be just passing fads, but others may develop and grow into a serious part of your life. You're learning what you like to *do* in life, and what God has on His heart for you.

SOCIAL: You'll probably prefer the company of guys. You will begin to like girls here, but more or less at a distance. You just feel so weird and awkward right now, that when you try to talk to a girl you feel like Charlie Brown. And girls can be really cruel right now, giggling at your squeaky voice and awkward looks. So for these years, girls won't outwardly interest you too much. You'll prefer to have your own gang of guys who share your interests, and run with them. Make sure your *closest* friends are *God's* friends too. You will be tempted to try out a lot of bad trips here: Experiments with drink, drugs, masturbation, dirty books, violence, and stealing. Be careful. What you learn here may deeply affect your future. Stay close to God, and don't let the crowd push you into a mold that Jesus cannot honor. Be a leader by sticking up for God's laws and His honor. Give your friends a solid example of being straight without being square.

SPIRITUAL: You'll be looking for answers — real answers. During this time, you may have a lot of doubts about the Bible, God, and Christian things. This is a hard time for you. You will probably be strongly tempted to just push Bible study and prayer into a small corner of your life because there are so many other things you  want to do. You'll think about Christian things every time you see God do something marvelous, but your spiritual life will be affected by the same plague of "change" that the rest of your life is going through during these years. Because your awkward feelings will be a hassle to you, you will wonder sometimes if you are really a Christian; if God really does exist; and if He can answer prayer. Don't be afraid of doubts, provided they are honest doubts. You may just bury them under a load of new things to do, and push yourself more into what you are trying out lately as your latest interest rather than think about them. But remember: God loves you; He understands you; and He cares for you. He knows the way you feel now. He is watching you, talking to you in a dozen quiet ways, saying, "My son, give me your heart." Learn it now; God wants to be a real *Dad* to you. Let Him.

Around age 16-18, STAGE TWO will seem to creep up on you over night until one fine morning — crunch! You'll realize you are more of a man than a kid — it's REORGANIZATION time!

PHYSICAL: Now your body actually *does* what you tell it to, with no unexpected side effects; you have added some weight and hopefully some muscle. You no longer behave like a one-day-old giraffe on stilts. Mother's china is experiencing months of relative safety from your destructive slips and trips of the past. You will have begun also to experience some important sexual changes as God awakens your sexual drives. You will begin to grow hair on your body, and will try your first shave (after first carefully cultivating your first beard and mustache). You will try to avoid as many cuts and nicks as possible so that you can seem to be an expert; but your pimples get in the way, and you may have a few accidents and go bleeding bravely to school.

By now you may have experienced some mornings when you find you wake up having wet your pajamas or sheets in a different way than when you were a little kid! Don't be alarmed; this is just God's special built-in release for the sexual pressure which your developing sexual drive generates. It will trigger every now and then, usually when you are dreaming, lying on your back. It is like the safety-valve on a pressure cooker that will save you from the temptation to masturbate (to trigger your own sexual function by stimulating your sexual organs yourself). Keep your mind pure and your thoughts clean; they will help you to keep a strong and energetic body. These are the sports years for those of you who are athletic. Your body is so together now that you can break records on court, field, and track. Go to it! Learn to use your skill and strength in physical disciplines for the glory of God.

MENTAL: Suddenly you'll be able to USE all that stuff you have been learning (hopefully) for the last three or four years! You will realize that you are really brilliant — a true genius, and you won't understand how it is that your parents could be so dumb on some things. Of course, you will want to show them how to do everything because you are convinced with your newfound, superior knowledge that you can save them time, energy, and also, impress them to no end. Hopefully, they will go along with you somewhat; still it may be frustrating for your Dad to have you show him the way to drive or fix his car, or for Mother to find you attempting to rewire her mixer for greater power. Be patient with them. When you are *their* age, you'll know what it is like; and it may surprise you in a few years just how much they *did* know all along. Let the Lord be "Boss" of your study life; let Him use your best subjects to make you "shine" for Him in class; perhaps He can take you to the top for His glory. You may be able to help other kids in your class who don't have as many correct answers as you do. It may lead to chances for witness.

SOCIAL: Suddenly you'll realize that there are girls everywhere! These can be wonderfully happy years in dating and learning to show affection and friendship — so long as Jesus is in control. Girls your age *are* interested in you now; you are, after all, looking more like a man every day; that creature next door you used to chase to pull her hair has suddenly turned into a demure, beautiful woman. You may get suddenly interested in poetry and music; now *YOU* are the one who is excited about dating, and that girl who was always there waiting to be asked out now has turned shy and hard-to-get. You will have a lot of dates, some of which will begin a little awkwardly, but end with you actually enjoying yourself. You will wonder about what a girl expects from a date at this time; let me tell you. She expects you to really take *care* of her, to treat her with honor and affection; and to be fun to be with. She will not usually mind being treated like a princess, and the guy who learns to do this will not lack feminine friendship! But guard *her* affection and *your* heart; don't let it degenerate into familiarity and then immorality. Keep your dates light and fun;

learn to mix with many different brothers and sisters during these years, and don't start exclusively dating just one girl, or it will put pressure on your life that could cause problems and possible real hurt for you *and* her later. Give your love first to Christ; then let Him make you a man of God who knows how to lead the girl he dates closer to Jesus. That's Bible dating; that's the way of happiness and peace of mind.

SPIRITUAL: Many of the guys you know are more or less skeptical about spiritual things. Some have begun to experiment with drugs; they are being pulled away from the Bible and into the mystic and occult worlds. You will hear various Eastern religious trips pushed around and fooling with seances, astrology, horoscopes, and Tarot cards will be common. These are all bad news; stay clear of them. You'll need a lot of real answers now, and you will be excited to find out that the Bible does not ask of us "blind faith." We are to "study to show ourselves approved to God." He will give you firm and clear foundations to stand on. He will give you a "wall to lean on that doesn't move." A lot of your friends will make bad mistakes now; the human ideas they gave themselves to will bring only emptiness, guilt, and bad trips. "Anything you do is right, as long as it feels good" will be the going philosophy. "Do your own thing as long as you don't hurt anyone" is another. You can have a comeback to this in that the last is the basic commandment of the Bible — PROVIDED no one hurts *God* either in their doing their "own thing."

You can't do your own thing if your thing is doing *you*. Stay clear of things that will trap and enslave you. Do it God's way with your whole heart. This is the time to really get your head and heart straight with God; this is the time to declare your independence from the hip crowd that is traveling Hellwards. Choices you make NOW will deeply affect your life and help shape your destiny. Do it under God. A solid and intelligent commitment to the Lord Jesus now may save your wholesomeness, your dreams, your future friendships, marriage, and ministry. Do it, with your whole heart.

Finally, you're on the last rung where you'll be moving out of your teenage years and into the adult future. Here are the times where you will finalize your life choices, and decide things that will take the rest of your life to live out. From 19-24 is stage THREE — *EXPANSION time* — where you learn to be BETTER at what you decide to do.

PHYSICAL: Your body will be mature. If you've liked sports, you'll be really advancing in it. You will have added some "steel" to those early layers of muscle, with the proper discipline and exercise. You may be becoming a leader with Christ in control. You're on your way to taking a place in the adult world of men, ready to carve your own personal notch in the destiny of this planet. You've made it so far — congratulations!

The next years ahead will be important to you in terms of *study*. They are the best years to learn in. Your head will be together; you are beginning to understand the world around you, and more than that, you know that you can actually change it. So give yourself to discipline, to training, to study during these years. Let God harness your sexual drives and channel them into a constructive energy for change. Don't waste time on foolish or harmful side tracks that will rob you of these critical study years. Between *20-25* are the *best years to learn* for a man; here you will have the most awake and flexible approaches to decide how you are going to do what you feel you *want* to do. It will be best for you to postpone any serious dating or marriage until you have had time to give yourself to the work of preparing for the future. The best years for a guy to marry are between *25-30*; by then, he has had some time to put his patterns together for the future, and he can use these years for added practical experience in his work. Don't get tied down to some nice girl just because *others* your age have, before you have had time to invest in *both* of your futures. And don't rule out the possibility of a creative *single* life; God sometimes has tasks that require a special man with unique gifts and abilities to serve him in a single ministry, especially if the task involves risk and danger in opening a new field for God and humanity.

MENTAL: Those high school friends of yours who never came over to God's side are almost all completely skeptical, or totally hung up in some other trip. Some of your more liberal or radical friends will be into power or political trips that provide a vehicle for their personal anger or hurt. You will have decided what you want to do, or are right now in the throes of "knowing God's will." Make your choices wisely; guard your mind from the poisons of vain philosophies and humanistic ethics. In the pages of God's Word, you will learn as much about freedom, love, meaning, truth, and value as you can intelligently handle, and more. Give yourself to the work of honoring God with your study life. "In understanding, be men."

SOCIAL: Here, your task before God will have competition from other pressures, like those of marriage, and possibly, competing job opportunities. Remember that all the time you give to these pressures will rob time from these critical development years. Discipline your life to put top priorities first. Do what God says first. Learn to relax in His love and to take your responsibilities with a smile. By now, the Christian outreaches which you were into in your early teenage years will be either specialized or curtailed; you will begin to learn how to bring the love of God into ordinary everyday life at school, or at work, or on the street. These are also years when you can build lifelong, lasting friendships, and cement relationships. Your interests will be narrower, your talents more specialized. You will be outwardly more calm and stable; although every now and then you will have flashbacks to those early uncomfortable years of trying to find yourself when you are put in a new and strange situation.

SPIRITUAL: Many of your unsaved friends will have begun to get hard, bitter, and very disillusioned about life's apparent emptiness. Some will have gone into hedonism, trying out the playboy philosophy for the empty, sensual thing it is; others will have hit the streets in mystical or violent trips; some will have  sacrificed their lives on the altar of education or business; others will have been locked into a system within which they feel like a helpless pawn because they did not have the direction that Jesus could have given them. It will be hard to reach young men here, but God is in the work of total change, and nothing is too hard for Him. You be available. Be a source of liberation, of wisdom from above, of quiet, practical, and dynamic leadership. Give yourself to the task of becoming a man of God in whatever calling God gives you. Be a friend with compassion and sympathy. Be a man who knows what true values are because he has listened to heaven; a man who knows where he is going because he is following the Light of the World; a man who speaks with authority and power because he knows Him Who is the Way, the Truth, and the Life. Ahead is your future and Earth's future. Walk into it unafraid because your Lord and Leader has already gone before you.

Growing up with God can give you years you will remember with thankfulness and joy. Build memories you can carry with gratitude into the future. Don't be afraid to wholly TRUST Him. Give yourself to Him as a child puts himself in the strong arms of a loving Dad; learn to know the beauty and simplicity in being a servant of the King of Kings. Let the whole world know that you are "one of THEM" — that you belong out-and-out to God — body, soul, and spirit. And take the reins of your world with the courage of the committed.

Be a MAN of God — in the way you look, dress, act, speak, and live. Be a real "I Timothy 4:12" person for God. The WORLD is yours for you and God to take together. And brother: God bless you — from the heart!

VIII

THE COURTYARD: Control

LET'S FACE IT!

Men and women were made for each other! From the first kiss back in Eden, the story of man, woman, and God has always been a "love story." God took Eve from Adam's side — and she has been very close to his heart ever since!

But let's face it — something has gone desperately wrong somewhere along the line. All around there are wrecked lives; broken homes and broken marriages, lonely girls and embittered, frustrated men; divorce and heartache. For every home hurt by quarrels and divorce, there will be children who learn how to hate and hit back. Maybe that's why, during the time it takes you to read this section, hundreds of people will have been robbed, raped, bashed, beaten, and murdered by *children* from homes like these. Maybe you can see why God is so concerned about marriage and dating.

Yet, we have more books on sex than ever before. We have more information on how to make-out; more data on being a sexy swinger; more products that guarantee that "if he kissed you once, he will kiss you again," and that your teeth will have all the sex appeal possible.

But we have left out God and His Word, and are paying a tragic price for it.

You may think, "I'm a Christian. I won't face this kind of problem." Wishful thinking! You will! Your world is becoming frighteningly like the morally deviate world into which the light of the Gospel shown some 2,000 years ago. God has given you a treasure, a power in sex. Every normal young person must learn how to control this flame, or it will burn out of God's time and out of God's place. Sex is like a fire. Fires are warm and wonderful on cold nights, IN A HEARTH and UNDER CONTROL; but that same fire *loose* in your home can *burn it down* with *you* inside it. Sex can be beautiful, fun, and genuinely lovely — but it must be the RIGHT PLACE, the RIGHT TIME, and UNDER CONTROL.

WHAT SEX IS

When God brought together the first man and woman, He told them, "Be fruitful, and multiply, and replenish the earth." Without this power of re-creation, our race would die out. Into each model of the human race, he placed mental, social, and physical differences, each designed to excite, compliment, and harmonize with the other. He sealed each system with the attractive power we call sex. Some people think God is *against* sex. But it is *HIS* IDEA. He *invented* it; He knows how it ought to be used. It is His gift to us, just as our eyes were given to see sunsets, our ears to hear music, or our noses to smell apple pie. Tremendous happiness can come when sex is rightly used because it is one of the deepest physical pleasures possible between a man and woman. Yet, because it is so deeply beautiful, it can hurt so *terribly* much if it is misused. It is like a sleeping tiger in your being: Wakened in fear or in rude shock it can maim, destroy, and kill; a tiger can only be tamed by the

Spirit of God, and brought instead to beauty, majesty, and pleasure. We must learn not to fear it, but to profoundly *respect* its power; if we forget, and play with it foolishly, we will learn the same bitter, tragic lesson as millions of others who have forgotten God's warnings! "Can a man take fire to his heart and not be burned?"

"I came back to reality with a sickening thud. Nothing was funny now. I wasn't drunk anymore. The party was over, and I felt sick, cheap, and dirty. It didn't make me feel any better to hear him say, 'Why on earth didn't you stop us before things went too far? You should have known what would happen. You could have called a halt at any time. But you didn't.'"

"My mother and dad just found out that I'm pregnant. They are so shocked they just won't believe it. I'm only fourteen years old. They just stare into space, and when they see me they break down and start crying. They say, 'It just can't happen — not to our little girl!' But it did happen. Now I don't know what to do or where to go. What future is there for me now? It happened so quick — it just wasn't worth it. Could you please find a home for my baby when it comes and could you please give me some advice before I lose my mind!"

"It's not so bad if you've never loved anyone because what you don't know won't hurt you. But if you're like me and have loved a guy before, what do you do when it has to end? I never used to have problems getting to sleep, but now I stay awake nights wishing I was back in some guy's arms again. And although I know it's impossible, I dream of all kinds of situations where he comes back; and we make up and it's all beautiful again. But it never happens, and the memories never go away and leave me alone . . . if you really care, give me some answers quickly. Please help me!"

Sex is an emotional hand grenade. Kids play with it, pull the pin, and it blows up so fast that their lives can be blasted and shattered almost without warning. When you first discover sex, it's a common temptation to experiment with it. Mothers who push their little girls to act "grown-up" by being "popular with the boys" don't help; the same mothers are the ones most shocked and hurt when their "little girl" comes home white, sick, and pregnant. Guys get gutter introductions to sex through friends, dirty jokes, pornographic novels, and pictures because their dads never had the guts to tell them the truth when they were little, and interested. Sexual things are so clouded in mystery today that many kids graduate from their "street" educations confused, guilty, ashamed, and dirtied. But God has not left us in the dark about sex. He has given us limits and guidelines to keep us happy and holy here. Here are some Bible guidelines.

HOW FAR IS TOO FAR?

Sexual sin begins in the mind and the *heart* (your choices). One Bible term is a Greek word that means "too much" or "excess" . . . the word translated, "lasciviousness." Used in a sexual sense, it means to turn on your sexual drive, to stir yourself up sexually-outside of marriage. Any thought or action that you deliberately make to stir your sexual consciousness (when that excited desire cannot be expressed in marriage) is *sin*. It comes from a choice of your will. The Bible says it is not the result of outside temptation, but comes from the heart. (Mark 7:22) No picture, book, or sexually-stimulating scene can "make" you lascivious. Feelings you have when suddenly faced with any of these temptations are not in themselves sin. Sin begins *only* when you find yourself *giving in*, looking again, or recalling the picture or memory to keep the flame under the fuse, Anything is wrong for you that turns you on sexually when you know you can't *afford* to be turned on.

"Too far" is ANYTHING that stirs up sexual desire in your heart outside of God's ways. Necking has been defined as " an exchange of kisses and caresses keeping both feet on the floor and all hands on deck." If necking turns you on sexually, it is wrong for you. There are true Christians who can *hug* each other and not be wrong, but there are other kids who can't even *look* at someone of the opposite sex without sinning. God knows your heart. Remember: It is sin in the sight of God to choose to stir up sexual desire when you know you can't go on with it and have God's blessing and smile. This one reason why masturbation (exciting yourself sexually by playing or fondling your own sexual organs) is wrong; it is simply another expression of the sin of lasciviousness.

HEAVY PETTING

"Concupiscence" is another big Biblical word which spells trouble in sex. It simply means to be overly hung-up on sex; to be bound by strong sexual desire; to be so controlled by it, that you keep going back to it again and again in your mind. The Bible sometimes translates it "lust." This is the word Jesus uses when he says to a man, "And I say to you that whosoever LOOKS on a woman to *lust* after her has already committed sexual immorality with her *in his heart.*" (Matthew 5:28) Concupiscence is the next stage up from lasciviousness; it is when sexual fires are really burning out of control. It makes a girl parade her body before guys and wear a sign in her eyes, "For sale-cheap. Slightly used, but still serviceable." It makes a man give the "x-ray treatment" to every girl's clothes who walks past. Concupiscence is no light matter before God. The Bible tells us it is one of the things He will judge in anger. (Colossians 3:5-6) We are not to let our bodies and minds be bound with this sin, even as the "heathen which don't know God." (I Thessalonians 4:4-5) Concupiscence is being so "turned-on" that you can't turn off.

NOTE: There is no break here for those who are already in this position. Suggestion . . . can't turn off without spiritual power from the Lord.

Lasciviousness leads to concupiscence, which is a Biblical way of saying that light-necking-with-more-in-mind leads on to heavy petting and deeper demands for physical gratification. And if you have begun either, it will do you no good to *pray while* you are doing it, asking God to "take away your desire" for sex! That is like crying, "Go out!" to a bomb while you keep holding the flame on the fuse. God *made* your fuse. It is *His* idea that it should burn down. But He put control in the hands of your will; and He expects you to yield that will and your body to Him, so you may give yourself to someone you love in *His* way and in *His* time. He can no more wisely rob you of your sexual feelings than He can happily make you a non-man or non-woman. The sexual bomb has a long fuse. It is lit by necking to lasciviousness and burns shorter in concupiscence. Heavy petting is just the first act to the final curtain — going all the way with someone — full sexual intercourse. God has reserved this only for the love and responsible commitment of marriage. So — don't pet at all. Don't even start! If you *have* started, stop now before it gets worse. If you have gone too far already, it is time you came back to God.

Petting CAN add to your life, it is true. It will add temporary feelings of excitement and pleasure. It will add, for a little while, the things that God wanted you to enjoy in marriage with someone you love. It will also add other things. It will add guilt and shame. It will add dirt to your reputation. It can also take away. If you are a girl, it can take away your boyfriend because after you go too far with him he may decide you are cheap and leave you. And think of all the other things it could add to your life! It can add jealousy, emotional volcanos of frustration and tension, deceit and bitterness. It can add memories of furtive meetings in sly and secret places; memories of watchful, hurried experiments, always filled with the fear of interruption or discovery. It can also take away your virginity; lead to pregnancy, break your parents' hearts; and get you married too soon or to the wrong person. God has reserved petting and sexual foreplay for only one place — marriage, and *marriage only*. If you want to mess around, you have a free will; but you will *not* be free to avoid the consequences. You will have to be ready to be part of the tragic statistics. And remember this: No sexually immoral person will walk in white in God's family. No Christian is a slave of sexual sin.

AND THAT OTHER PERSON

DEFRAUD is another Biblical term. It defines the sexual sin which begins when you involve someone else. It simply means to *turn-on someone else* sexually when you know you can't go through with it. The original word means "make a gain of" or, in the passive form, "to be taken advantage of." Any time you set out to inflame someone's feelings, when you deliberately choose to make them fall in love with you so that you can use them for selfish reasons, you defraud. It is possible for you to unwittingly hurt a brother or sister deeply by giving them the impression that you love them in more than a "brotherly or sisterly" way. Anything you do deliberately to make that impression is fraud. Used in a sexual sense, defraud means to make choices and actions to turn someone else on when you know good and well it is wrong to do so. You cannot take advantage of someone else's trust and affection without getting into deep trouble from God. He says, "Don't go too far and defraud your sister (or brother) in *any matter;* because the Lord is the avenger of all such. We also have warned you before; God has not called us to uncleaness but to holiness." (I Thessalonians 4:6-7)

Don't let the fire burn outside of God's control and limit marriage. You will not be able to safely stop it, and it can burn you sometimes badly, deeply, and irreparably. Sex without God is full of dangers. Do it and you will not only get yourself and others into trouble, but you will be in trouble with Heaven. Sexual sin has terri-ble penalties. Ask any Christian who has already been down this one-way road. Once you get into this fire, only the power of God can help you out of it. And even then, it may leave scars that you will never erase in this world.

Sexual experiments never promote friendships before marriage; they throw in barriers to happiness that will crop up later. God never intended sex to be merely physical; rather, it's the complete surrender of the whole person to another, a "soul sharing." Anything like this outside of marriage is debased and dirtied. Besides, most normal males want a bride who has not been petted and pawed and used by previous possessors. And girls who stay true to their finer instincts will have the courage to turn down a thinly-disguised seduction offer flat. Carry your sexual life wisely; prize it; and never sell it cheap on the auction-block of one night's surrender. It's not worth a life time of regret.

There are, of course, other dangers. There are the exploding *venereal disease* rates: New forms of sexual disease that respond to no known forms of treatment, that can strike a life through only one casual contact, and then crop up again in latter years to cripple with sterility, disease, insanity, or even death. Then, despite contraceptives and other techniques for preventing unwanted conception, *pregnancy* still happens to tens of thousands of unmarried mothers, and that's not counting those who HAD to marry, who were forced by their circumstances into something that left their lives permanently scarred and resentful. Even with modern contraceptive methods, nothing is really 100% safe, even when it is used the right way. And then, of course, there are the girls who take a pill the hour before they go all the way with their boyfriends, and bravely hope it will *stop* what God took all His genius of design to make work.

Sexual intercourse is never just physical, never just bodily union. It is spiritual too, the union of two souls. Every girl's chastity (sexual honesty, cleanliness of mind and body) is interwoven with her moral sense, her nervous system, and her physical well-being. She may give herself expecting to be rewarded with devotion and love, but the guy, who may be only interested in self-gratification, is soon off in search of new experiments with other girls. The conscience-wound she gets may never heal, and she suffers shockingly. Or it may harden her so that she will never again be sensitive to all the fine, high dividends that sex in its right place — Christian marriage — pays.

God doesn't pass laws for fun. He has given us sexuality, but it can get out of control. There are no bells built into you, other than your conscience, that will ring and will tell you how far to go without hurting yourself or others. Once you light this flame, it can catch hold of both of you so fast that you will be almost powerless to stop what happens. Think back. A lot of people made the same excuses as you could, but they still ended up trying to patch back up the bits of their blasted lives.

God must go on your dates. He will help you run your date-life in joy and beauty. He won't be in the way and will not intrude into your happiness; but He understands and knows your weaknesses and what will trip you up. And He will keep you pure, by His Holy Spirit, provided EVERY-THING (and I do mean EVERYTHING) is put in His hands! Read this verse of Scripture:

"Your body is the *temple of the Holy Spirit.*"

Read it *again.* Your body was not made to be a slave of sexual sin. Your body was made to be a home for God. Will you give it to Him? Will you let Him keep your heart clean? "Listen, son of Mine, to what I say," says God, through His writer of Proverbs. "Listen diligently. Keep these thoughts ever in mind; let them penetrate deep within your heart, for they will deliver you from the shame, and give life. ABOVE ALL ELSE, GUARD YOUR AFFECTIONS. For they influence everything you do in life. Spurn the careless kiss of a prostitute. Stay far away. Look straight ahead; and don't turn your head to look . . . RUN FROM HER! Don't go near her house, lest you fall to her temptation and give the rest of your soul to the wicked . . . lest afterwards you groan in anguish and in shame when syphilis consumes your body and you say, 'Oh, if only I had listened! If only I had not demanded my own way! Oh why wouldn't I take advice? Why was I so stupid? Now I must accept the consequences.' Drink from your own well, my son. Be faithful and true to your wife . . . For GOD IS CLOSELY WATCH-ING YOU." (Proverbs 4:20-5:21)

DATING RULES FOR CHRISTIANS

(1) Never date just for the sake of it. If you really want to count for God, ask Him to use each date for His glory. It could mean an opportunity to witness, a future contact, a soul saved. Let Him use your date — He wants "in" on EVERYTHING you do, right?

(2) Tell your date what you have planned, or find out from him what is happening before you do go out. If you have nothing special in mind, and too much time on your hands, you could put yourself in a situation where you will be under a lot of pressure. Don't be too general on a date; work out EXACTLY what you are going to do. Shorten the time you are going to spend together if you have nothing special in mind; if necessary, set yourself a deadline to be home in and KEEP IT!

(3) *PRAY TOGETHER* on your dates, or at least in private, committing the whole time to the Lord. Be carefree, but sensible — ask Him to keep a rein on your emotions, so that you won't let your heart get ahead of your head.

(4) Whenever possible, *DOUBLE DATE,* or go out with a whole family of Christians. When there is just two of you, and too much time, look out for danger. Don't mix too much with the wrong crowds except to reach out to them in love and witness; it can be too easy to conform your standards to those around you. Avoid places where you'll be alone for any great length of time with your date. Watch out for parked cars!

HOW TO STAY OUT OF TROUBLE

Ninety percent of your temptations on a date will be overcome if you remember and practice two simple guidelines:

GUYS:

(1) You will have problems being excited by a *LOOK*, since most of your prime temptation will come visually; so GUARD YOUR EYES. Keep a "Job's covenant," and you will keep the doorway to your mind and emotions.

(2) You will give a girl a problem by *TOUCH*, so KEEP YOUR HANDS TO YOURSELF! If you take care of your eyes and hands, you will not be burned on a date.

GIRLS:

(1) You are going to give a guy problems by the way you DRESS, so watch it! Don't dress to stir lust in your boyfriend; dress as if you were going to be ushered into Heaven right on your date, and Jesus will not be ashamed of you. Help keep him from temptation by the right clothes. (I Timothy 2:9-10)

(2) Keep a "hands off" attitude with your date. It may be hard to say "No" but you must. No heavy necking or petting can develop this way. If your boyfriend doesn't understand because he doesn't want to understand, repeat it a couple of times, then use this "emergency" prayer:

Extend your free hand from your shoulder, pull it back behind you, Then offer up a quick petition thusly: "Lord, give me strength for this task!" Then *slap him hard!* If he doesn't think your action was very scriptural, show him Ecclesiastes 9:10 — "Whatsoever thy hand findeth to do, do it with all thy might."

IX

GUESTROOM: Friends

And now, the guestroom. A special place in the home, where friends who are staying with you have their own little place. Let's look at your friends and friendships.

"God so loved the *world*" — that means EVERYBODY! So have many friends; not just those few "close" ones, but others you meet at school, church, work, or sports. God wants us to mix with people so that we can influence them for Him. People need to know that Jesus is the "Friend of sinners." How can you have more friends?

Perhaps you have had *trouble* making friends before. You may be shy or not feel that people will like you. It is true that some people in the world will never like you. If you live for Jesus there will be selfish people, runaways from God's love, that will not want to know you too well (in case you get through to them about their lost souls). You will meet bitter people who have been hurt and do not trust anyone. Christians don't expect to be popular with everyone. But the Lord Jesus had many friends. He was a supremely friendly, understanding person. You could come to Him and always be sure of a welcome.

The world always has a funny idea of Christians. They think of us in terms of being too far out on religion; not tolerant of other faiths; not able to enjoy a little "fun" in life. The world always has a miserable picture of Christians. But remember, that is not why the Pharisees criticised Jesus. They said He was the "Friend of publicans and sinners." Sinners liked Him too much. Jesus had a knack of mixing with people and building them up even when he was putting down their wrong.

HOW TO BE MORE FRIENDLY WITH PEOPLE

(1) *First, get properly clean before God.* If you are holding on to fear, guilt, anger, or worry, you will give off bad vibes wherever you go. If you have been *hurt*, forgive. If you have things to get *right*, do it. You must be clean or you will always be afraid to meet people in case they spot your secret sins. Remember the Christian is to be totally clear. He is to be as transparent as a mountain stream. God has given you the promises and power to be free. Go to Him first and get your heart clean. This is the first step to making friends. Do it *now!*

(2) *Learn to forget yourself.* Shyness is only a form of pride. One of the big reasons people don't make friends is that they try too hard. They do crazy things and say too much to be real. People get "scared off" when you try too hard to be friendly. You can never be natural by thinking all the time, "I wonder what he thought of what I just said; I wonder if she thinks I look okay; I wonder if he can see my pimple?" RELAX! Be natural. Be yourself, pimples and all. Be a loving "just-who-you-are."

You can do two things to help conquer shyness. First, think of some time when you really felt at home, relaxed and at ease with someone. Carry it in your heart and mind. Remember how you felt. Think about how easy it was to talk, to say things that people listened to and liked you for. And when you meet someone new, first bring back to your mind that feeling of happiness. Practice living in your attitudes of that time, and you will find your tenseness draining away; you will be more relaxed and free.

One of the best ways to stop thinking of yourself when you are trying to make friends is to change your way of thinking about *them*. Instead of thinking what you can GET from the friendship of this person, think of how you can GIVE to them. Think of what GOD is doing in their life; how you can be of help to them; what you can do to serve them in Jesus. God has been dealing in some way with this person; you are there to help Him in His work. Don't worry about what THEY might be thinking of you. Concentrate on THEIR needs. This is the way to project a real spirit of friendship; in thinking about their needs you will forget your own shyness.

Another way to make friends, especially with those who are HARD to like, is to make a *LIST* of the *good* things you can find out about them. Write down what you might find attractive, or pleasing, or praiseworthy in them, even if they are full of faults. Then PRAY for them; ask God to *bless* them, to *help* them. *Thank God* for the things you have found out that were nice about them. You will be surprised at how much you can find if you open your heart! Ask Jesus to love them into a solution of their problems *through you* if possible. Make yourself available to Him for it.

MORE BIBLE WAYS TO MAKE FRIENDS

(1) *Do what Jesus said*, LEARN THEIR NAMES and remember them; then say a friendly "Hi!" to them, even if they don't say it to you *first*. Go out of your way to make this a habit of your life. To help you remember the name of someone you meet, say it *back* to them when they tell you. Use it straight away in your talk with them two or three or more times. Repeating it will help you to remember. People like you to use their first names. Write it down after you have met them to remember even better. They will almost always like you if you remember their name; it means you

found them important enough to remember. God knows *our* names. If we want to be Christians whom people like, do the same thing with them.

(2) *Show yourself friendly*. (Proverbs 18:24) Every Christian must go out of his or her way to help others in studies, in jobs needing doing, in introductions. You can *choose* to be a friend. Think, "If Jesus loves this man or woman, I can love them and care about them too. If I can help them, I will *offer* to. God has left me here to serve, and this is someone I can show His love to." (Proverbs 17:17)

(3) *Look out for the lonely and neglected*. The world is filled with people that others pass by without even looking at. Make it your ministry to say a kind word to at least one new person every day. All around you there are people who have no friends, with no one to care for them or even notice. Some have been hurt, and have hurt others in  return so much that they become sour, bitter, and driven away all their friends. You be a light in their darkness. You speak kindly to them despite their rude ways. Some you brush past today may go down the road to suicide, death, and hell tonight. Will they say, "No man cared for my soul?" (Psalms 142:4) Be one of the first to meet newcomers to church, or school, or work. Don't just hang around with your own little clique.

(4) When you *do* talk to people, *don't* talk about yourself. Talk about *them*. Be really interested in them, but not nosey; give them the feeling you enjoy being with them. Look them in the eye, and smile. Ask them about *their* problems, their needs, their work. Learn to be a good *listener*, learn to make people feel *important* when they are with you. Learn to build them up and make them feel worthwhile. Of all people, the Christian knows that man *is* worth something. We know that people are not nothings. We know they are

important and valuable, because they are made in God's image. We can love them because God made us all, and we are related by His creation. *This* lonely man is made in your Father's image. *This* lonely girl is made a tiny finite copy of my great Creator's love and wisdom. I can love them and make them feel important, because they are important to God and, therefore, to me.

MAKING FRIENDS WITH CHRIST'S FRIENDS

Of course, your *closest* friends will be *Christ's* friends. Although we will be free to find out what most people love and want to do, the problems they have, and what God is doing in their lives, our closest friends will only be a small circle of people. They will be the ones we REALLY ENJOY sharing things with; those we spend a great deal of time with. Close friends are people we can share our deepest feelings and hopes with, people we can really fellowship with. We feel more free to help such friends grow spiritually by throwing in our efforts with them in some task for God. We can expect them to lovingly show us if we are doing something wrong, and they will expect us to do the same thing. We cannot have too many close friends; there is not enough time to share everything with many in one lifetime. But this "inner circle" will be close to our hearts, and we must make sure they are Christ's friends.

UNITY in prayer comes only by a close, common bond of understanding, affection, and friendship. Jesus put His team of disciples together on that basis. Your closest friends should be people of *similar interests*, people who *think* like you in most situations. They should also be ones with a similar *spiritual level of growth* in God. They should be ones with whom you can share new discoveries of the work and Word of God in your lives.

Sam Shoemaker has pointed out that true unity is not just *two* people who agree in the same things; it is more like a *pyramid,* where two people form one line, God forms the third corner of the base, and the common task or ministry they have together forms the peak. When we walk with God together, under His control, and doing a common task He has set us, we will really begin to know the joys of divine friendship. With friends who are Christ's friends, we can know God's love demonstrated every day.

POPULARITY AND YOU

It isn't good to be *too* popular! The Bible warns us of this many times. "He that makes many friends does it to his own destruction; but there is a friend that sticks closer than a brother." (Proverbs 18:24) "Woe unto you when all men speak well of you." (Luke 6:26) The world will hate the true Christian because of the truth he bears. But there is no reason why we shouldn't be looked up to and liked AS PEOPLE. Here are a few more things to help you be more popular:

(a) Admit your mistakes cheerfully.
(b) *Listen* to what others say, even if you are right.
(c) Be a good WINNER and a good LOSER. Don't moan or brag.
(d) Make a "bad habit" list, and ask God's help to fix them.
(e) Don't call older people by their first names.
(f) Think of ways to make other people feel important.
(g) When talking with people who disagree, *agree* with them as much as you can.
(h) Avoid saying a direct, "No, you're wrong!" Use, "Well, that's interesting, but have you ever thought of it this way?" Use facts, not will power to win an argument.
(i) Never put someone down by "proving them" wrong. Always make it easy for them to change their minds about what they said gracefully, so they won't feel like Charlie Brown. If you are not sure *where* they stand, give them the benefit of the doubt. Say, "Well, you probably didn't mean (state position) did you, because . . . (give facts)."

DATE DIFFERENTLY — DO IT GOD'S WAY

God made us different! We can have friendships of many kinds that are but a shadow of the friendship of God. Some of the loveliest friendships of all are those that can develop in our early years of getting to know the complimentary sex: It is wise to know the differences God has put in men's and women's personalities so we can understand how to date *God's* way and understand how the "other" thinks:

PHYSICAL: Apart from fairly obvious sexual differences, God has made most men physically stronger than women. Now, I know there are exceptions; I know all about the woman who weighs four hundred pounds, has a black belt in karate, and can kill a moose with her breath! But usually, God made a man *stronger* physically so that he can protect his girl and take care of her. Now, girls turn physically into women sooner than boys turn into men. When most guys are playing marbles, running in gangs, and flying kites, girls their age are desperately falling in love with their English teachers. This means a girl can have a woman's *body* but a little girl's *mind*. It can lead you girls into dating older guys. It can also lead to trouble unless you know what's happening and get ready for it. That's why some fathers freak-out when they discover their little girl is going out somewhere with an older guy. Dads have been around. They know what is happening. Listen to them sometimes. They may ground you and you may not understand the reasons. *They* may not either; but maybe it's because they care about you, or even sometimes because they remember something of their own past with some guilt and regret.

MENTAL: There are usually *mental* differences between men and women. Now wait! Before you girls slam this chapter shut and huffily join Women's lib, let me explain. This has nothing to do with intelligence. A lot of women are smarter than guys I know. The Book of Proverbs is filled with warnings to men about the wiles of the strange woman, but never feels it necessary to warn women about strange men. Girls can be every bit as brilliant as any man around, as far as *thinking* is concerned. The difference has to do with the WAYS God designed us to USE our intelligence. There is a basic difference between the *way* a girl thinks and the way a man thinks. A MAN operates like an I.B.M. computer. He is matter-of-fact. He is a line-on-line, precept-on-precept person. He thinks logically in straight lines, adding fact to fact to get a conclusion. His thoughts go like this: "1 . . . 2 . . . 3 . . . 4 . . . 5 . . . 6 . . . and THEREFORE: 'bing!' . . . SEVEN!"

A *GIRL,* on the other hand thinks less like a computer than she does by a feminine form of "extrasensory-perception." Her thoughts come in bundles from all over the place, as God has made her to be intuitive and inspirational. She has her "vibe" collectors out everywhere, and she prefers to run by *their* messages than by "normal" channels of logic. Her thoughts may go like this on the above problems: "1 . . . ah . . . 4 . . . 3 . . . ah . . . peep! . . . therefore, SEVEN!" This, of course, totally blows her boyfriend's mind. He can't ever understand *how* she got from one place to another; how she came up with the *right* idea from all the *wrong* reasoning and all the wrong sources, or how in the world she can get the right answer from all the wrong logic. Give up, brothers! You'll never do it. God probably didn't intend us to understand. He just made us so we can enjoy it, and be amazed and amused at the mystery of a girl.

Now this is important. These two basically different ways of looking at things make each sex superior to the other IN THE ROLE GOD HAS GIVEN THEM. The *GIRL* is superior to the guy in her way of thinking when problems of life require an inspirational, intuitive, unstructured approach. She is good at seeing the whole picture, even if she isn't sure how to put it together. The *guy* is superior to the girl when a problem needs logic, fact, analysis, and detail to solve it. He is good at putting a lot of little bits together in the right place. The girl tends to see the whole forest at once; the guy tends to go in and explore each tree. If each stays in the roles God gave them, He can bring maximum blessing to their friendship or later partnership. Right through the Bible, beginning at creation, God has set up two roles for both sexes: The *girl* must *INSPIRE*; the *man* must *LEAD*. Each one needs the other, and both need the Lord. This is God's pattern. When we do what we were designed to do, we will find maximum happiness in our friendships with each other, in our courtship, and in marriage.

MEN ONLY — HOW TO LEAD IN GOD'S LOVE

Because you men are supposed to be leaders, here are some rules for growing hair on your chest. God has placed a real responsibility on your shoulders to guard your girl.

(1) *Get Smart.* The Bible says "In understanding, be men". If you are to be the I.B.M. computer, "study to show yourself approved" to God. A girl likes to have the man she depends on to be informed, and to know how, and why things work. Be wise.

(2) *Get a sport.* Develop your physical body so that you will be strong enough to take care of her and protect her. A girl likes her guy to be a shelter to her. Pick something you can enjoy and really work at. "Bodily exercise profits a little." Even if you look like the "before" picture on a Charles Atlas advertisement, do the best with what you have. Keep yourself at least fit and healthy, even if you are a little skinny.

(3) *Be a gentleman.* The Bible tells us, "Be courteous to one another, (kindly affectionate) in love preferring one another." (Romans 12:10) Watch your manners. Give your girl the respect due to a woman of God. Remember, the *King of Kings* is her Father. Treat her like the princess she really is. I am sure you will find she will not mind at all.

(4) *Don't tell lies!* "Speaking the truth in love." (Ephesians 4:15) Never lead a girl on to think you care for her more than you care about *others* if it is not true. Girls get hurt too easily, and want to believe you too much. Don't you dare indulge in some mild power trip just to feel that some girl is under your "spell" even though she means nothing much to you. If a girl DOES get hurt, that hurt will go deep because of the way she is made; and she will not forget it easily. No guy has the right to say to a girl, "I love you," unless he is *ready* to say in the NEXT breath "Will you marry me?". If you can't say the *second,* don't romantically say the first.

(5) *Be a MAN OF GOD.* If, you have one epitaph on your tombstone, strive to make it this: "Here lies a *man of God.*" Unless you know how to love God and serve HIM wholly, you will never learn the tenderness, care, and concern that makes a guy a worthwhile leader, sweetheart, and one day, husband. If you are going to *lead*, be a leader where it counts — spiritually. Brother — *hear me now.* NOTHING counts more than your walk, your personal, daily walk with Jesus. It will save you and every girl you befriend from heartbreak, trouble, and wasted, irreparable years.

FOR GIRLS ONLY — BEING AN INSPIRING WOMAN

You have been given the role of an inspirer. Use some of these tips to help you do what God designed you for, and see how much more lovely and enchanting you become to him.

(1) *If you are smart, don't show it off.* No brother wants to feel like Charlie Brown. God doesn't want you to put on some dumb blond (brunette or redhead) act; but remember, he is supposed to be the leader and your job is to inspire him. (Proverbs 31:26)

(2) *Don't gab.* Sister, here is a secret. If you want things to talk about, ask HIM what HE thinks. Learn what it

means to *build a man* up with admiration. A girl wants to be loved; a man likes to feel *admired*. You can do it by just asking a few questions and a lot of wide-eyed listening. Don't just listen to his *words*; listen to the MAN who is saying them. Many guys are "beautiful," but really shy. You may bring him out by just a few well-caring  words; smile a lot; admire greatly, and say little. He will love you for it. Be simple and honest like a child. If you are serious about marriage, which will not be until you get out of your teenage years, you should talk about your walk with God, his feelings on a ministry, home, children, finances, and parents. But *don't* gab. Keep your life a lovely, intriguing mystery to him. (Proverbs 11:22)

(3) *Be fragile.* Let HIM be the strong man. HIM Tarzan! YOU Jane! Have you ever seen a weedy little man call his 200-lb wife, "My little baby?" Now, she learned the secret of "being fragile" in his eyes. It is not just how you *look*; it is an *ATTITUDE*. Don't go around killing your own spiders. Let HIM do the strong-man stunts. Things like this make a woman feel like a man. Generate a dependent, a helpless-little-girl look. That's the kind of girl a man loves to be a leader for. (I PETER 3:3-4)

(4) *Dress and look like a woman.* That woman must be *all girl* and *all lady*. Stay away from the tough-as-nails look. God has given you a marvelous attraction; you are a woman, and you are GOD'S girl. Use these facts to the full. Don't dress cheaply or lewdly, so you look no better than a tired hooker. God is your Father, the Lord Jesus is your brother. *Dress* like it. Be clean, simple, and sensible. (Deuteronomy 22:5, 11)

(5) Be a *WOMAN OF GOD*. There is nothing more beautiful and mind-blowing to a man who loves God than a girl who is *really* in love with Jesus. There is no better source of

looking beautiful than living in the joy of perfect obedience to His will. Learn to be someone *Jesus* can be proud of. You will understand what God means when He says, "Delight yourself IN THE LORD, and He will give you the desires of your heart." Make God happy with your life and love, and He will open the door to your dreams coming true. Be happy just in Him, and your life will turn on in beauty and radiance.

Men, in your outings with your sisters, *you* take the lead. Decide where to go before the Lord. Commit each date to God in prayer. Date so you will lead the girl you date *closer to Jesus.* You don't really know how to love in God's way until you have led a girl closer to Jesus because of the time she spent with you on your date.

Girls, you are to live so close to the Lord that by your *very life* you will draw him closer to Christ. *Inspire* him to be a world-changer for God. That is the Christian way to date. You have not loved him deeply enough until you have drawn him closer to Jesus by his having spent time with you.

"Not only in the words you say,
Not only in the deeds confessed;
But in the most unconscious way,
Is Christ through you expressed.
Was it just a beautiful smile?
A heavenly light upon your brow?
Oh no — *I felt His Presence*
When you laughed, just now.
For me, 'twas not the truth you taught,
To you so dear, to me so dim,
But when you came to me,
You brought a sense of Him;
And from your eyes He beckons me;

And from your heart, His love is shed;
Till I lose sight of you as you,
And see the Living Christ instead."

TESTS OF TRUE LOVE

Do you *really love* your boyfriend or girlfriend? Test out your personal friendships and love life against this "John Three-Sixteen" examination:

(1) *"FOR GOD . . ."* All true loving must be done FOR GOD. We don't know what it means to love until we can unselfishly put the Lord Jesus first, and because of our love for Him, really *care* for the ones we meet. Christian love must happen within real Christian fellowship and witness. Our love is to be holy, set apart as sacred under God. The man or woman who has never given up their selfish ways has never really learned to love at all. Everything they do is to make *themselves* more happy. Then, if *others* fit into their own interests and pleasure, they will make them happy too, if it suits them. And this is in no way real love. You don't know the real meaning of love until you experience God's love. This love is the control, the guide, the underlying care behind all true Christians' dating actions and words. Without it, there will be nothing but surface interests, friendships, or sexual attraction. *Honestly now* — are you dating your friend for GOD'S GLORY? Did you start this friendship to please and honor God, or is it just a sidetrack of the Devil and his crowd?

(2) *". . . SO LOVED . . ."* Real love, God's love, is special. It can *feel* more deeply than any other kind of love; but it is NOT just a feeling, it is tremblingly alive to all the joys and pain of the world around it; but it is NOT just a sensitive compassion. Love is far *more* than feeling; it is also intelligent. No one who loves with God's love ever "falls" in love; that is *romance*, and while romantic feelings are beautiful and exciting, they are not enough to hold a marriage together. The love of God is first of all a WISE CHOICE for the highest happiness of the one loved. Love is an act of the *will*; love is something you *do*; it is sure and careful.

Girls, promise the Lord that you will bring your boy-friends to Him for His approval, and not just rely on your feelings to tell you whether he is alright to go with. It is too easy for you to just let your emotions run your heart, but you cannot afford to do it if you want to be God's girl too. Men, is your *first* motive in going out with this girl to bring her closer to Jesus? You may feel strongly about her; but remember, feelings can come from any girl who is interesting and attractive, who shows some interest and attention to you. But you can't marry or live with *everyone* who does this. Enjoy your feelings, but do not let your affection run ahead of your mind and will. Love takes time; it thinks before it commits itself. If you trust your feelings, you may be hurt very deeply. Trust God . . . learn what it is to "so love." Don't blow your purity and your future over a supercharged gland. If you love God, don't cheaply sell the body or the affections He has given you.

(3)". . . THE WORLD . .". Love wants *everyone* in on its happiness! Love has a great heart. If you love your friend with God's love, you will want the world to know about it. Do YOU love like this? You can tell shallow, counterfeit affection; it is selfish; it wants to keep to itself and for itself. If you love with true love, you won't try to exclusively control your friend's life just because *they* care for you; you won't be envious or worried if they spend time with others, because you will trust them. Leave the one you love FREE

to make their own choices before God. True love cares for all creatures and doesn't willingly inflict pain. It is not partial to select few; it is color-blind. Do you mind sharing your love with others? Do you want to tell the world about the one you love? If you are envious, you don't love with God's love. If you can't witness or pray with your date, you don't love them. Now, do you trust your loved one enough to share them with others? Do you admire them so much that you can be sure they will not let you down in any situation or with anyone else at any time?

(4) "... THAT HE GAVE..." True love always wants to *give gifts*. Love works out ways to make others happy all the time. It would help everyone the same way if it could, but it does whatever it can. Love, from its very nature, will deny itself to promote a greater good whenever it is wise to do so. You can *give* without loving, but you cannot *love* without giving. Love is first concerned with *God's* happiness and others' needs; it only thinks of its *own* needs in the context of these. Love never uses another person as a tool for personal pleasure or popularity. Now, do you want to *share* with your love? Do you want to give gifts, even if it costs a lot to do it? When you see her, do you think in terms of what she would like? When he calls, do you just naturally have something for him? Is he worth your giving him the full devotion of your heart? Do you think she deserves the slaving labor of your hands?

(5) "... His ONLY-begotten Son ..." There is always a *cost* to true love. Love cost God His Son; love cost the Lord Jesus His life. Love means you are willing to give up *everything* for the one you love. When love rules, you choose things for their true value, and not just for personal gain. Love counts the cost, but it doesn't keep on counting it. Now, how much do you love *God*? Do you love Him enough to even say good-bye to one who has grown in your affection deeply if you find that they will interfere with God's will for you? Do you have that unreserved trust in God that leads His true child to say, even if it hurts for a little while, "Your will be done, Father?" This is a costly test, but you must be prepared to take it. Do you love God enough to GIVE UP any earthly love? When you pass this test, you will know the joy of God in the midst of pain and heartbreak.

(6) "... That whosoever BELIEVES in Him ..." Love involves *absolute trust*. To fully love you must first trust yourself and the other person. Love has faith in the other person's character and integrity. Love hardly even notices when others do it wrong; love is able to live with another person's failures and weaknesses because love knows

the other person for what they *are* and is willing to *be* known for its own true character. Love doesn't seek to impress or pretend. Ask yourself: "Does it encourage me on to greater, more lovely things to think that she would admire what I am doing? When questions come up, do I quite naturally think about what *she* would say?" Or, do

you think a great deal about *him,* little one? Whatever you are doing, is he never far away from your thoughts? Do you implicitly *trust* the one you love, anywhere with anyone? This is one of the reasons why God puts limits on premarital sex. To hold back from sex before marriage with one you love and want to marry is a proof that you trust each other. And when you trust, you can really love, because you won't be afraid.

(7) ". . . should not perish, but have EVERLASTING life." The Bible says that when you love someone, you will be loyal to them no matter what it costs. You will always believe the best of them, continually standing your ground in defending them." (I Corinthians 13:7-8)

Love is an eternal thing. True love will *last,* regardless of the trials it will face. Do not rush then in deciding who you want to marry. Love will always have time; it is never in a hurry. It will be harder for you girls to wait on God and trust that He will arrange for you to meet and marry the one who will bring you the greatest happiness and usefulness. But if He wants you to marry, He will. Here is the hardest test; are you willing to *wait*? You can test that very easily in your date life. If you cannot discipline your life to wait for God's time, you have not learned what it means to love with God's love.

If you are getting *serious,* give your relationship the *TIME-TEST.* Get to know the other person really well — not sexually, but personally. Do you have a *good time* together, no matter what you are doing? Do you have the basic heart-feelings about Christ and the work He has called either of you to do? Are they able to fit together? Do you quite naturally think of the future with him? Do you see her standing with you as you stand up for God in your destiny to come?

If you think you are serious enough to get engaged, but are not sure, give yourselves a *SEPARATION-TEST*. Now, it is not good to have long engagements. It is too much of an emotional and physical strain on you both. Once you are sure, you should marry soon. But in the "deciding" time, spend a period of time apart from each other; say *six months*. In Bible days, if a man wanted to marry a girl, he announced his intention to do so, then left for a year to raise money for his future home. At the end of the year, if he still felt the same way about her, and she him, they invited over all their friends and relatives and made it formal and permanent. After a long party, they simply lived together as man and wife. This was Biblical marriage. If you are going to spend the rest of your life with this person, you can afford to give it two tests: *Time* and *separation*. The TIME-TEST will show you if your love is genuine and deep, or only a feeling of attraction that may pass when you see someone that looks prettier or nicer. The SEPARA-TION-TEST will help you know the difference between excited, romantic feelings and serious, loving commitment.

You will want to *WRITE* a lot during the separation test; it will give you both a chance to know the one you love without their physical attractiveness getting in the way. Bring all the trials and tears you may have at this time, all the tests to God. If it is of *Him,* it will *last;* what *God* joins together, no man can break apart. Love "endures all things." What is of Him will last forever, and you can trust Him to guide you in this, your happiest and most important human decision.

"No voice is heard, no sign is made,
No step is on the conscious floor.
Yet love will dream, and faith will trust,
That He who knows our need is just.
That somehow, somewhere, meet we
        must.
Alas for him who never sees,
The stars shine through the cypress trees;
Who has not learned, in hours of faith,
That truth to flesh and sense unknown,
That Christ is ever Lord of Life,
And love can never lose its own."

X

LIVING ROOM: Family

This is the big room, that all-important room which tests your readiness to help others, your growth in God, and your ability to minister to those that are in need. It is here, more than any other room in this part of your house, that real "living" must be shown, day by day.

WHAT GOD SAYS ABOUT YOUR HOME

"Honor your father and your mother; that your days may be long, and that it may go well with you in the land which the Lord your God gives you."
(Exodus 20:12; Deuteronomy 5:16)

There is an old song that says, "Be it ever so humble, there's no place like home." It doesn't mean what it used to mean to a lot of kids today. There is no place they can really call "home." They feel the loneliness of Neil Diamond's song "I Am, I Said" when he sings "L. A.'s fine, but it ain't home, New York's home but it ain't mine." Home for thousands of young people is a living Hell — where they stay until they get old enough or mad enough to leave.

No one really knows what goes on in your home as well as God. His eye is in every place. He sees all that happens. Every wall is transparent to Him. Whatever is carefully hidden from the eyes of the crowd is not hidden from Him. He sees the lies, the bitterness, the greed which goes on under a cover of virtue. He sees the kid who steals  from his parents; the one who is shooting up, or masturbating in his bedroom; the ones who use their house as a place to have "free" sex. He knows all about the fights, the quarrels, the drugs, and the drinks. He sees your family as they really are. But still God CARES about your home, even if it is as bad, or worse than I have described it. He really understands when you feel afraid, sad, or alone instead of in peace and happiness at "home." And He wants to change all that is rotten and wrong in your family and make it right and clean.

If Satan can wreck your home, he knows he can turn you on a path that leads straight to Hell. Under a hundred covers, in a thousand subtle ways, he can tear up your family. The Bible says that when a man and woman marry, they "cleave" to one another. The word means to "stick" like to paste or glue or cement together. When that joint is ripped open, it tears and hurts. Satan pulls at this love-tie. He works on your parents when they are tired or ill or bound by habits, hoping to slash apart their love and split your family in two. He tries to turn brother against brother, sister against sister, parent against child, father against mother, with stupid little differences or big, horrible past memories that keep growing into explosions of hate and bitterness. And too often he has done it! And it is OUR sin that has given him the open door to move in and make our home into Hell.

Your nation is only as strong as its homes. When the family is ruined, the nation is on the way to the end. It is the foundation of order. When homes begin to fall apart, riot, rebellion, and anarchy will stalk the streets. Civilization is murdered when the home is put to death. Kids have walked out from their homes, dads have left by the hundreds of thousands never to come back, mothers have dumped their kids on the doors of adoption agencies and just split. If something is going to be done for the world, it must begin AT HOME. And that means YOUR home!

How do you think GOD feels when he sees your family? He first planned the home for happiness. He began the first marriage, blessed the first family. From the start, He chose to use the home as a picture of how to love and obey Him. He gave laws for the home, laws that have been broken by our generation with terrible re-  sults. Every family that breaks apart hurts more people than we can realize. If each family had only four children and the kids make the same foolish mistakes their parents did, within a hundred years (four generations of twenty-five years) over six hundred and eighty people will be messed up. And every hurt that happens in every heart is felt in all its pain by God. Here are His laws to keep our homes happy and what He planned as a Father for those families of His children:

(1) *Parents should love Him with their LIVES* as well as their lips. Too many religious parents are just phony church people without a real experience of the Lord Jesus. They turn kids off totally from real faith. Too many radical young people today come from church homes — even preacher's homes. Not always is this their parent's fault. But often parents have not done what God said. Do your parents spend real time with you? Have they taught you to work and play and love and laugh? God wants them to be a source of strength and guidance. Your home was meant to be a place of peace, love, and security. And God longs for it

to be like that even MORE than you do. He wants your parents right with Him. And now, a question for you. Are you helping Him to affect their lives by doing your part?

There is a set of directions in the Old Testament that almost every Christian has heard about and read. It is called — no, not the Ten Suggestions — but the Ten COMMANDMENTS. And only one of them has a built-in beautiful promise with it. It is the one special command for kids. God knows how hard it is to obey and honor some parents. He put a special promise with His command. The law is "Honor your father and mother." The promise is "that your DAYS MAY BE LONG and that it may GO WELL WITH YOU."

In this command God promises us two things if we obey. One is a LONG life. The other is a GOOD life. If we break this command, we set in motion laws of judgement which will bring us two tragedies. The first is a rotten life. The second is a shortened one! You will not live long, and you will not live well. Fail to honor your parents, and you will get bitter over their faults and sins. That bitterness will lead you to reject all authority. Loss of respect for any guidance or control other than your own will open the flood-gates to all kinds of sin. That sin will bring guilt and with guilt, loss of respect. No self-respect means that you will no longer love yourself. And when you stop caring about yourself, the door opens to suicide. The Bible says, "The eye that mocks at his father, and despises to obey his mother, the ravens of the valley shall pick it out . . ." (Proverbs 30:17) The result of dishonor and bitterness over parents? A short life and a rotten one. No, we cannot afford to break the laws of God. Even for your own sake, if not for God's or your parents, you must obey the law — "Honor your father and mother."

(2) *The Lord Jesus must be FIRST "Boss"* of your home. DAD is to be next, then Mother in that order. The rest of the family are to be subject to them. Dad is to lead the home under God and provide for all its needs. This provision is not just "things"; God expects Dad to take care of his wife and children of course; she should not have to work for the bare necessities of the home. That is HIS job.

God says, "If a man provide not for his own, and especially for those of his own family, he has denied the faith and is worse than an infidel." (I Timothy 5:8) But provision also includes love and time with his wife and children. It also means time with God on behalf of his family. If parents fail to meet the spiritual and emotional  needs of their families, as well as the physical needs, they may lose them. The Beatles underlined this when they sang, "She's leaving home after living alone for so many years" while her parents are saying, "We gave her most of our lives; sacrificed all of our lives." Dad must spend REAL time with the kids, not just give them "things." Mother is to be the INSPIRER of the home. She is to stand behind Dad and encourage him on in his work and leadership; be there when she is needed for comfort and advice. (Ephesians 5:22-23; Colossians 3:18-19; I Peter 3:1-2; Titus 2:4-5) Now if this is NOT true of your family, do you really want it to be? Are you willing to obey God so that He can show you what you can do to begin to affect it?

(3) *You are to love, honor, and obey your parents as you would obey the Lord.* Now I did not say that. The same Holy Spirit Who gave us the Bible said that in God's book. (Ephesians 6:1-3; Proverbs 23:22; Luke 2:51; Colossians 3:20) And He did not say "Love your parents if they are nice to you," or "honor them if they always do the right things." He just said, "Obey them in the Lord, as to the Lord." And this doesn't mean that if they are not Christians you can tell them to go jump in the river! It does mean that as long as you live in their home, and as long as they ask you to do anything that God doesn't forbid in His Book, you are to do it for Jesus' sake.

Did you ever think that maybe God could USE your unsaved parents to speak to you? It is easy to blame them for all their wrong. But what if God is using them to point out to you your own lack of love for people who are rotten? If love involves meeting others' needs, and not just expecting them to meet yours, do you really love your parents? It is easy to love people who are lovely. Anyone can do that. But it takes a person really changed by Jesus to love people who are not. Do you believe that God could speak to you through your unsaved parents? Do you see that every rotten thing they do could be just another chance to show them the love of God? The question is not what have they done to make you feel ashamed of them, or hurt over them; the real question for you is, "Have I obeyed God by doing what they asked me to even when it didn't fit into my own plans?"

Loving your parents doesn't mean feeling good about them, especially when they do wrong or cruel things. Remember, love is a choice; you can choose to do right even when you feel like becoming the same as them, and returning evil for evil. No, loving them doesn't mean becoming like them. It means swallowing your pride  and hurt and doing what is best even when it is hardest. Honoring them means respecting their God-given authority over your life, even when you think you know better. Obeying them means doing what they tell you, even when you would most like to do something else. God has ways of dealing with problems. But as long as you take things into your own hands and fail to do it His way, He has two problems — your parents and YOU. He will do something in your home. But let it happen His way. Begin on His side. If anyone can win your parents to Jesus it should be you.

IF PARENTS GO WRONG

Maybe your story is like that of the fourteen-year old girl who said, "I don't hate and don't want to hate my Dad; but he started kissing me in a funny way when I was 12; I didn't understand it then, but it got worse; finally my Mother found out and threw ME out of the house. I don't understand; why did my Mother blame me? They said they were going to call me for Christmas; but they haven't, and if they don't call soon I'm going to wind up hating them both forever." Or like Charlotte, who went out with a bad kid at school, and then found herself pregnant at fifteen. Shocked, hurt, and deeply ashamed, she went home to try to tell her parents what had happened. Her Dad put his finger in her face and called her a dirty little tramp. She has never gotten over it. "I don't hate him now" she said; "but give me a year and I'll hate the ground he walks on." OR the fifteen-year old who bitterly admitted, "My Dad's going to leave Mom. They don't know what I know, but just you wait. The day he walks out on us, I'm going to become the dirtiest little hippie the world has ever seen."

HOW DO YOU LIVE WITH PROBLEM PARENTS?

There are no easy answers to problems like this. Every kid who has lived in the streets knows what it's like to have problems at home. The world is filled with rotten parents. They come in all kinds. But remember: Parents are just people, and people have problems. And some people have far worse problems than others. If you have given your life to Jesus, stop looking at your parents like they were a problem, and start looking at them as people you have a chance to help where no one else probably can help. Mario Murillo tells of the time when, in the middle of his big home problems, he threw himself on God, and the Lord spoke to Him. It seems as if the Lord looked down through time and knew that in the last days homes would fall apart. So He said, "In the last days, I will pour my spirit upon all flesh." That spirit is the spirit of adoption. God thought, "If no one will take care of the kids in the last days, then I will. I will be a Father to them. I will make them My children. If no one will love them, then I will love them."

ALCOHOLIC PARENTS: Perhaps one or both of your parents is a slave to alcohol. You have felt the shame of having to move bottles to get in the house; the agony of having friends come around when your Mother or Dad was there drunk; the pain of having them fight in drunken rages. Perhaps God has called you to help your parents. There are reasons why they are alcoholics. Part may be medical, but another part is spiritual. You must take steps to really love them. First ask their forgiveness for not being the kind of kid you could have been. Tell them you love them and are praying for them. Gain their confidence by being trustworthy and by not showing revulsion over their problem. God loved *you* when *you* were a mess. You do the same with them. Ask God for His gift of peace in your heart, so you can work from His calm strength. Ask them if you can help them in any way. Contact the A. A. or other Christian social welfare agencies that can help them with this problem. Try to bring your parents in contact with a minister or man of God who can counsel and help them spiritually. And *care* for your parents, by cleaning up for them, choosing their highest good despite the pain and the grief their alcoholism will cause you. They need Jesus very, very much. And He can sometimes touch them through the fog of a ruined life and bring them to repentance and new life.

ATHEISTIC PARENTS: Maybe your father is president of the local rationalist society, or your mother specializes in giving lectures in atheism. But despite this, you have discovered the love of Jesus is real. Remember; most people who call themselves atheists have not done so because they calmly sat down and thought through  evidence on both sides. Usually it is because they have been hurt in some way with some kind of church connection. Every rampant atheist I know has had bad contacts with some kind of religious situation. Pray for your parents.

Never allow yourself to get bitter over *their* bitterness, or you will find yourself becoming just like them. Don't *argue* about faith with them. If they argue with you over your faith, never raise your voice or fall into the trap of getting angry over their words. Speak quietly. Spend much time in the Bible. Don't antagonize them by deliberately trying to "show them up" by doing spiritual things when they can see you. Demonstrate your changed and different life *practically* around the home. Your aim is to show them *by your life,* that giving your life to God, has made you a better person who loves them more because of it. Love will sometimes win them when all the arguments have failed to move them one step closer to God.

BRUTAL DADS: Some parents learn to take out their frustrations and hatred on kids by beating them brutally. When the Bible says "Honor your parents," it doesn't mean to let yourself be bashed around until you are beaten senseless. Now, if you have done something wrong that deserves punishment, take it like a man or a woman. But no Christian has to suffer cruelty silently, without being able to call for any help or protection. You have the right to rebuke a parent who is cruel. Tell him, "Dad, stop it. When I am wrong, I know I ought to be punished. But be fair. It's not right to take out your own problems on me. I am your son/daughter. I want to love you and respect you. But I can't do it when you are cruel." (Go first when he is over his anger. Tell him then.) Be sure you first apologize for not being the kind of child you should have been. Then tell him that you will respect his wishes and will do whatever he asks you to do which is right; but if he will not be fair, you will leave the house until he calms down.

Try to find out why your Dad is so cruel and angry. Does he trust you? Does he do this because he has made a mess of his own life, and can't find anyone else to take out his frustration on? And if you can, try to help him by bravely walking with God in the midst of his rotten life. Love him — care for him — but be firm. And stay out of his way when he gets in a bad temper. Tell him that if he gets angry, you will leave until he has cooled down, to help him not hurt himself, God, or you any more.

BLACK MAGIC: Spiritism and occult activity in the family are growing problems. Many parents are involved with satanic activity expressly forbidden in the Bible. Your house may be filled with demonic powers and fear because of occult activity your mother or dad is involved in. You must steadfastly REFUSE to take part in any way. The occult arts are like a deadly, contagious disease; a small contact contaminates and begins to infect others. Resist the temptation to experiment in any way, or to take part in anything that involves occult activity. Go to a friend's house while your parents are doing things connected with the devil. Take a number of Christian friends with you and pray in and over each room in your house which you can. Have your friends make you a special subject of prayer to guard your mind and spirit from the wiles of the enemy. Get rid of any music at all which is vaguely connected with the world. Fill your room with Christian music, and STAY AWAY from all hard or acid sounds, as well as the depressing "downer sound" of blue and minor music. Learn to praise and pray in the Spirit, NOT FOR YOURSELF, but for others. Demonstrate the reality of a life lived in the love and power of the Holy Spirit. Know in a real and practical way the power of the Holy Spirit. "Greater is He that is in you than he that is in the world." Refuse to read any books on spiritualism, even for fun or curiosity.

CARELESS PARENTS: Sometimes you have parents who think they love you so much they don't want to set any limits on your life. That is foolishness. God loves us; but that is why He gave us limits. When we know what is right and what is wrong, how far we can go without causing trouble, we have freedom to build and create and grow. If your parents say they "care so much" or, frankly, just don't care at all what you do, YOU care. Set yourself limits. Ask God for help to learn the fruit of the spirit which is called "self-control." Set yourself a time to be home, and *be home* by that time. Regulate your own hours of play and work. Read Christian books, and biographies which will give you the model for living that your parents have not been able to provide.

CHURCH-GOING, but non-Christian: Some parents aren't really evil sort of people; in fact, they may go to church every week. But you know they don't really love Jesus, because it is not much more than a social or reputation thing with them. Don't condemn them, or try to preach to them about their "hypocritical lives." They  may not know anything more than what they have been into for the last fifty years. At least they are trying to set some kind of religious example, even though you may have learned more about Jesus yesterday than they ever have in their whole lives. Live joyously around your home, be helpful, and sing Christian songs while you wash the dishes, clean your room, and make the bed. Bring home (after asking) friends who are sold-right-out Christians, just to fellowship and to meet your parents (again, not to preach to them to get them "properly saved"). Your job is to provide an example of genuine Christian love and reality. Let *God* give them the rest of the message.

DIVORCED PARENTS: Maybe your parents have split up for good. You may be staying with your Dad, or with your Mother, or maybe you have moved away into a separate flat or apartment. *Don't* develop bitterness; and if you already have, get rid of it. Ask forgiveness of both parents separately; this will help you clear your heart of hurt. Do things *for both* of them out of love for them. Spend an equal amount of time with them, whenever you can, and whenever they will let you or want you to. Don't *take sides* with either of them; no matter how wrong one of them was, don't side against that one and stick up exclusively for the other. Love them both, the lovely and the unlovely, the loved and the unloved one. Maybe God will use you to speak to both of your parents about the love of Jesus. Maybe they can both make a new start one day, because they both have a new heart. And if they are remarried, don't hold grudges against your step parents. They are legally and scripturally the ones you are to listen to, because the court has given them custody. Your true parent can advise you and you can go to him or her for counsel, but he or she has no power to command.

DIFFERENT FAITHS: Perhaps your parents belong to two different faiths, and that has been a source of tension to both them and you. Treat them the same way as you would divorced parents, because a difference in faith is like a spiritual divorce. When you witness, stick to the main issues; don't get off into minor doctrinal differences.  Be positive about the love and harmony you have found in Jesus. And if possible, go to a service or two with either or both of your parents, with the promise that they will both come to one which you attend. Then really pray for both of them to find spiritual unity in Jesus. If one parent is a Christian and the other isn't, buy books which will help the Christian one to win the other.

DEAD PARENT: Maybe one person in your family has died, and your mother or father is alone in trying to bring you up. It is sometimes harder when it is your Dad who has died; Mother has a double responsibility to provide for the needs of the home and to bring you up as well, with any brothers or sisters you may have. You carry more than your share of the load. Look for ways to get extra work and help support your mother. Help her carry the load, by being responsible and trustworthy yourself. Give her extra love, because she is alone now, and it is harder for her. If your mother is a church woman, have her take her needs to God in the weekly prayer-meeting. It is the church's responsibility to help out widows and those who are in need. You make sure you belong to a body of believers who follow that Bible command. Have some Christian men in the church pray weekly for your mother, that she will have the wisdom and strength to make the right decisions in raising her family. Lighten her load as much as you can.

OVERBEARING MOTHER: We are usually close to our mothers, but sometimes they can try to live their lives through us. It is an old trick of the Devil to convince a mother that her children, especially her son(s), need her more than they do anyone else in the world, even more than God. Our mothers are very important in God's pattern of training in the family; they can give us both love and inspiration in God's order. But if mothers get too possessive or too domineering, a lot of pressure is put on their children. When mothers have problems like this, boys are pressured towards homosexual or Hitler-type living. You must take steps to *re-build* your father's leadership in the home. In the presence of your mother, say things that honor and uphold your Dad. If your mother asks you to do something which is a family decision, do it; but if it comes to a *choice* between what your mother says and what your dad says, follow your father's directions, each time, unless it is a command to specifically commit sin. God has put Dad in the home to be a leader. Help him do it. Resist the temptation to undercut his leadership by working on poor old Mother to give in, when Dad has said "no." Go to your Dad and ask him permission first when both parents are home. But don't put your mother down while you do it. Just smile, recognize her authority, and say, "Right Mother; I'll just have to check with Dad first, to see if he thinks it's O.K."

OVER-STRICT: Have you ever wondered why some parents seem to be far too strict on you? Put yourself in their place for a little while. Why would you be strict on your kids? Maybe it is because you remember what *you* did when you were a kid, and you are getting uptight now because you recognize (or *think* you recognize) the same sort of things you used to do? Maybe some parents remember their own lives as kids with a measure of fear and regret. In the Billy Graham film "The Restless Ones," April Harris, a young prostitute with an alcoholic mother is being questioned by her mother as to how she got the money to buy an expensive dress. (The dress was bought with money she got by selling her body.) Suddenly April turns on her mother and says, "What did *you* do when *you* were young that makes you so suspicious of me?" Silence! Remember; sometimes parents are too strict because of either guilt or fear. You must learn to BUILD trust with them. Do exactly what you say. When you tell them you will be home at a certain time, be home earlier if possible. Do all jobs you are given. EARN their trust. It will take time. But if you can prove you are trustworthy, you may find them relaxing their strictness a little.

SUCCESS-CULT: Sometimes your parents seem to have their hearts set on you being a "success." Now this is also natural. It is only right that parents should expect their kids to be some kind of credit to the world, and to be successful. But sometimes they don't know what success is. Biblical success is living in God's ways and by

His principles. Sometimes, "success" to parents means fame, fortune, and power. That may not be the way God is leading you; but you cannot go to war with your parents over this. Tell them you are happy that they want you to succeed. Say you want to be useful and worthwhile to your world. But try to *re-define* success so they can understand that your values are not just based on how much money you will have, or how well-known you will be. Point out that a lot of crooks are wealthy and well-known. (Matthew 6:33) Say you are working to have a successful character, and a good reputation, which is far more worthwhile to you than just to have a great deal of money which you can't take with you when you die. Give some creative alternatives to their own "plans" for your future. Explain simply that you don't really feel too interested in the thing that they want you to do; but you will go along with it for as long as you can, until you are absolutely sure what you want to do, and know how to do it. And thank God for your parents. At least they care enough about you to worry about your life. Some parents have never done that at all.

Now pray for these who hurt you. Don't pray, "Oh Lord, judge my rotten father. Really smash my hypocritical mother. Deal with them for me, Lord. Wipe them out if it is your will." Really see your parents with all their hurt, frustration, rage, and sin being loved by Jesus. See Him reach out His hand and touch their own hurt hearts. The Bible says, "Bless them that curse you, do good to them that hate you, and pray for them who despitefully use you and persecute you; that you may be the children of your Father which is in heaven; for He makes His sun to rise on the evil and the good, and sends rain on the just and the unjust." (Matthew 5:44-45)

The final step for you in forgiving a family which wrongs you is to begin to list ways in which you can help the ones hurting you. Are there things which they need that you can work to buy for them? Are there jobs around the house that no one likes doing which you can step in and do for them? Are there things which they have always asked you to do which you have not done before? Then do them, in the Name of Jesus! The Christian way is to *will* their highest good. And you will find something strange happens to your heart. As you do these things, step by step, God will restore the love that you once had for them. It may even bring them to Jesus. And if you can't be an effective testimony to your family about the wonderful change the Lord can make in a life, who can?

Go now, when you have determined in your heart to empty the files of your resentments; clear out all records against the ones who have hurt you; wipe completely clean every account of wrong done against you. Forgiveness means to purpose that you will never bring up old wrongs again, to them, to others, or to yourself — or to God. Go now, no matter what they say, or how they react. Perhaps you can say something like this:

"Dad, something happened to me that should have happened a long time ago. I've just seen how my .... (You fill in the blanks with the thing you've done which really hurt your parents most) has hurt you. I know I've wronged you in this and I want to ask you, 'Will you forgive me?'"

"I think that God is proud of them
That bear a sorrow bravely. Proud indeed of them
Who walk straight through the dark to find Him
And kneel in faith to touch His garment's hem.
Oh, proud indeed of them who lift their heads and
shake
The tear away from eyes that have grown dim
Who tighten quivering lips and turn to take
The only road that leads to Him.
How proud He must be of them. He who knows
All sorrow and how hard hurt is to bear
I think He sees them coming, and He goes
With outstretched arm and heart to meet them
there
And with a look — a touch on hand or heart
Each finds his hurt strangely comforted."

XI

THE OFFICE: Authority

Here is the room where all your executive decisions are made and carried out. All of us have the ability to have *authority*. The Bible says, "He has given us the privilege of urging others to come into His favor . . . and God has given us this wonderful message to tell others . . . for we are Christ's ambassadors." How is your authority?

MOBILIZING OTHERS

People respect authority when it is backed with truth and love. A lot of young people today have been hurt by authority based on force and fear, deceit and falseness. God needs people to demonstrate what *true* authority is like. You ought to have some authority in your life because you know the Lord Jesus; and He is the Way, the Truth, and the Life. You know *who* you are. You know *why* you are here. You know *where* you are going. You *do* what you say you are going to do. You mean what you say, and you say what you mean. Sometimes God will give us a latent leadership ability that we can develop for His glory.

If you are put in charge of a group of people, follow these guidelines for leadership:

(1) *Gain and earn their CONFIDENCE*. Be the kind of person people can trust. Treat them like the people they are. Be "boss" but don't be bossy. Be firm without being hard.

(2) *CONVINCE* them that they are *needed*. Don't do everything yourself, even if you think you can do it better. If you have a team, let them do something worthwhile.

(3) *Give them RESPONSIBILITY*. Be SPECIFIC and DETAILED. Don't leave anything to just "happen." Tell them exactly what needs to be done, how to do it, and when to do it. Never overlook little details that are important. Don't leave anything to chance. And let them make suggestions sometimes; they may come up with better ways of doing it.

(4) *COMMEND them on a job well done*. Find something nice to say about them before you do any form of constructive criticism. You will never, of course, criticize without love. All criticism must be done out of a loving choice for that person's highest good.

(5) As they learn to handle *smaller* tasks well, *increase* their responsibilities. This is the Christian way to grow in both faith and life. "He that is faithful in that which is least, is faithful also in much . . ." (Luke 16:10) This is WORK, but it is well worth it.

TAKING LEADERSHIP POSITIONS

Every Christian whom God has gifted with ability to speak out for Him ought to aim at some form of leadership position in work or school. This will do two things; it will earn for you the right to be heard as a Christian and give you a platform for a greater outreach and testimony to those around you.

YOU MUST GUARD AGAINST:

—Yielding to the pressures of the crowd — compromising your testimony for popularity.

—Getting too bigheaded and bossy; you must learn to carry your authority with humility.

—Getting too involved, and forgetting your responsibility to God — why He put you there.

—Forgetting the purpose of your office, and using it to feed your own image and ego.

THE PATTERN

(A) THE LEADER:
You are the most important part of this plan for leadership. E. M. Bounds said it: "The church is looking for better methods; God is looking for better men." What you are on a day-by-day basis forms the platform for what you say.

(1) *Be RIGHT-ON*. Dress well, look good, and feel good. Let God own your body so it is strong and serviceable. Groom so that you have the maximum influence with the crowd you want to reach. Obey God's health laws to keep you feeling fit and alert.

(2) *Be OUTGOING*. Christians must be marked by a noticeable absence of hangups. Be positive, outgoing, and cheerful. That ought to come naturally from a clean heart and life, and a real concern for others in God's love. Don't be afraid to speak up for what you know is right, or to take a stand on issues of moral or spiritual value.

(3) *Be CONSISTENT*. Your *Doorways to Discipleship* program will help you here. It is designed to give you an overall balance and harmony in your life. Christians ought to be the most natural, stable and trustworthy people around. Always strive for the SAME

OFFICE in every organization you are in. If you want to be president, always run for president; if you want to be secretary, always aim at being secretary.

(B) *The OBJECTIVE:*
Know what you want to do and why. It is important to have as good a knowledge of your goal as you possibly can. Make it a point to be highly informed. Anticipate objections and problems; draft out rough solutions for them before you run into them. Decide what position you feel God wants you to have. Fix it clearly in your heart. Then set your goal, and work towards it with courage and faith. Use Doorway 6 to help.

(C) *BEGIN YOUR CAMPAIGN:*

Never put off for tomorrow what you can do today. Don't wait until you are older to run for a position of influence. Begin now!

Make as many *friends* as possible without compromising on issues of truth or value.

Develop *loyalties*, by being the kind of person who can be totally trusted.

Take *responsibilities* as they come; up be thoroughly dependable in doing them.

Get *involved* in all important school functions where you will not have to compromise your testimony. Make it a point to be a totally-involved person where the action is. If the competition is keen, run for a *lesser* office first and excel in it.

TAKING OVER A SCHOOL FOR CHRIST

(a) *Begin an early-morning prayer meeting* with all who really want to see God move on your campus. Here you will claim individual people for Jesus. Ask God to lay on your hearts ONE PERSON that He wants you each individually to speak to Him about. Set this up in a home near the school, and make it early enough to discourage all the hangers-on who are only along for the ride. You want a small, committed core.

(b)   At the end of the meeting, hand out a *"witness tool"* for the week. It may be a button, a poster or a ticket for a Christian outreach. Another week, it could be a book geared for evangelism like the *Cross and The Switchblade,* a new tract, or New Testament everyone will use during that week at school. Close *early*, don't drag out the meeting.

(c)   At school, every Christian will pray that they will have a chance to talk to the person God has laid on their hearts. Then *everytime* the *bell rings* for class changes, for lunch, for assemblies, *each Christian* will send up a short, sentence prayer for the one God has laid on their hearts. This means each day there will be scores and scores of prayers going up for unsaved people. Then open your eyes and look out during the day for an opportunity to speak to the one you have been praying for! Don't push — just *wait* for it. It will come. If you don't see them that day, repeat it again the following day.

(d)   Every Christian must prepare to be a *leader* in the thing he or she is best at. All Christians in *athletics* will go on the track, field, and court to play for God. All the Christians good at *study* will become the best thinkers in their class, with the most contributions to make in their chosen fields. All those with *artistic* or dramatic talent will pray that God will make them outstanding and work for it. The one difference between the Christians and the rest of the school who also want to lead will be this; when asked the secret of their lives they will speak for the *glory of God.* And each Christian revolutionary will use his gift and leadership to help others for Christ's sake until they too become involved in this "magnificent obsession" for Christ's sake.

(e)   Every Christian will be on the lookout for the *lonely* and *rejected* in their school. The worst and the most ignored will find that they have at least one person who ...bout them — and that person is a Christian. In your ...r meetings, ask God for the hearts of the worst kids in s....ol. If *they* turn, their change will make a great impact in your school, and your revolution is on.

(f)   Make available the *best Christian books* you can lay your hands on for your task force. The *Youth Aflame* Discipleship Manual, *The Jesus Person Maturity Manual* and the *Jesus Person Handbook* will all be of help. *Campus Invasion, the Jesus Book* and cartoon tracts will be helpful for evangelism and for witness. Have your kids buy out of their own pockets the best follow-up material and tracts for new Christians they can get so they will use them wisely. Challenge them to TITHE their TIME — 2.4 hours a day for study and prayer and witness in the will of God.

(g)   Love the kids in your school so much that you are willing to DIE for them. They will feel it, and deep-down it will make them respect your stand and listen. It will make you tender when you warn; put tears in your reproof. *But do not hedge on the conditions of true discipleship.* Lay it out straight with those who are interested in following Jesus. Tell them that to become a Christian means that they must give their *everything*. Do not try to make it easier than Jesus did. He has promised life only on HIS condi-  tions to be totally honest; to see, hate, and forsake sin, and all selfish ways; and to give Him everything we have and are. Don't be soft here or your revolution will die. One person who makes an easy "decision" that does not work will turn off at least seven others by his false testimony. Every kid must give to God all they have, and are, or make it plain that they cannot call themselves a Christian. He invites us not to a party, but an execution. (Luke 14:25-33)

(h) Make sure that all you do flows out of a *REAL CARE* for the hurt God feels in His heart over the sin of the kids in your school. No matter what your *methods* are, no matter how good your *message*, unless you have GOD'S *motives*, He will not bless your work. Why *should* you take your school for God? Is it because kids are overdosing on drugs, or tripping out so badly that they are committing suicide and something must be done? Is it because it's time that Christians woke up and really witnessed before the church becomes pushed aside and ignored; because both teachers and students are agnostic and unbelieving? Is it because Jesus is coming soon; because the Communists may soon take over the world? All of these may be true, but *none* of them are the reason why you should take over your school for God. The reason is this: GOD IS BEING DISHONORED by the sin of your school! When you let your heart break with the things that break God's heart, you will see a spiritual revolution in your campus.

You *can* take your school for Christ! Of course, not everyone will give in to God. But you can know that the vast majority of your school has not only had a chance to hear about Him, but a chance to give their lives to Him; and that many more than you would dream will turn their backs on their past and sell out to the Lord Jesus. *It can happen* — in *your* school. It can happen *now*.

There will be a cost. The best things always have a price, and spiritual revolution is no different. Remember young Lenin, who "thought and dreamed revolution twenty-four hours a day." So must the Christian revolutionary. Every thought must be brought into captivity for Christ. Every class must be an opportunity for a word in the name of Jesus. Every talent must be bent towards spiritual awakening; every sport made the vehicle of Christian witness; every leadership position the target for takeover by a disciple of Jesus! Nothing less than wholehearted commitment to this task will suffice. We must "seek first the Kingdom of God and His righteousness." (Matthew 6:33) God must begin His revolution with His kind of people. It must begin with YOU. It must begin NOW. In the Name of Jesus, go and DO IT!

THE MARKS OF A LEADER

George Verwer makes these penetrating remarks on being a true leader for Jesus:

> "The Lord Jesus said, 'Follow Me and I will make you fishers of men.' (Matthew 4:19) This is but one of the many places where He exhorted His disciples to follow Him. He would say the same to us, His twentieth-century disciples. The burning desire for each of us should be to follow Him. We would not follow men or men's ideas, but Christ and His ideas. We need men of God who have been "chosen of God" to take on definite responsibilities of leadership in  both practical and spiritual realms. Only time will tell whether the young fellows and girls carrying responsibilities of leadership have what is necessary to see victories day after day in this type of work. And the question that will make the difference is whether or not they are *followers of Jesus*. Some individuals might feel they should be carrying some position of leadership. To such individuals, I would say, 'Then learn to follow; learn to take orders from someone else; learn to bury your own plans and ideas, allowing someone else to make decisions which you will wholeheartedly carry out, and soon you will find yourself being asked to MAKE decisions. There is no room for the person who has all the answers. We must take the position of learners for a disciple is a LEARNER. A disciple is always willing to be taught. He is always willing to listen to

another's point of view and to esteem it better than his own. He does not covet a position of leadership, but only desires to be a disciple of Jesus. You must not expect that you will always agree with your leader, or see in him perfection; for remember, he is as you are, just a follower of Jesus.' "

"It is in your power to make or break your leader. To ruin his leadership, just do the following . . ."

(a) Don't do what he asks you to do unless you *FEEL* like doing it.

(b) Don't do what he asks unless you *understand* and *agree* with it completely.

(c) *Forget* to do the tasks assigned to you to do.

(d) Do what he asks, but *grumble* and complain about it to yourself and others.

(e) Make him *explain* in detail why he wants it done before you do it.

(f) Take everything he says as a *personal offense* and bear grudges in your heart.

(g) Never bother to clear the air in a misunderstanding with him.

(h) Point out to *others* in the group the mistakes and failures of the leader.

(i) Present to the others "prayer requests" concerning what you feel is wrong with him.

(j) Constantly express *doubt* that his decisions are wise; always expect the worst.

(k) Point out *constantly* that *you* are right and that you have more experience and a superior spiritual life than your leader.

(l) Be sure to say, "I told you so," when he makes a mistake.

(m) Never take into consideration cultural or other differences which may lead your leader to think and act differently from you.

(n) Assert your *authority* over the leader, especially when he isn't around.

(o) Constantly *correct* him and give him advice, especially in the presence of others.

(p) Don't take time to *pray* with him, and miss as many devotional times as possible so that you can never seek the face of the Lord together.

(q) Be especially sharp to catch all his driving faults and make sure that all of the group knows about them.

(r) Keep him up *late* at night talking about his mistakes and how you feel the team should be led, coupled with discussion on minor devotional differences.

If you practice one of these points, I can almost guarantee that you will succeed in destroying both the unity of the team and the effectiveness of the leader. All of us, therefore, should take as our motto Matthew 7:12. Let us have fervent love among ourselves, for love covers a multitude of sins. "Therefore all things whatsoever you would that men should do to you, do ye even so to them; for this is the law and the prophets." Let us realize that there will be problems, disagreements, and differences of opinion; but that by triumphing in the life of love and faith, all these things will but strengthen the team. (Hebrews 12:1,2)

MAINTAINING TEAM UNITY

(a) Let the leader *know* that you are standing with him and are willing to help in any way possible.

(b) *Do what he asks* you to do, never failing to carry out even the smallest job.

(c) When you see something that *needs* to be done, do it without being asked.

(d) If your leader does something that you feel is a definite sin, then go to him *alone,* in love and meekness, and present it to him. If he repents, then rejoice together in the victory. If he does not repent, then take two or three of his friends and go to him again. If he still refuses to repent, then everyone should be told, or the central headquarters of your work notified.

(e) Keep in mind that many of the greatest leaders in the history of the world have made some of the biggest mistakes. Your leader might not make so many mistakes if he were home doing *nothing* (at least not such obvious ones); but the fact that he is moving out for God makes it almost certain that he will make mistakes, for only those who attempt something can make mistakes.

(f) Get together as much as possible to *pray* for your leader, and constantly seek ways that you can help bear his burdens, and so fulfill the law of Christ.

XII

RUMPUS ROOM: Activities

The place where all the action is — the rumpus room! Here is where all the fun and recreation takes place in your house. How are your activities under Jesus?

CONVICTIONS: OR COMPROMISE?

Sooner or later you will have to make a choice between what is *right* and what is *popular*. Every Christian has to. Whether you stick up for the truth or not will depend on how much you really know about right, wrongs, and your love for Jesus. It's easy — very easy — to avoid "rocking the boat" and just let the world around us squeeze you into its own mold. But we cannot afford to be plastic. God says, "Love *not* the world, neither the things that are in the world; if any man love the world, the love of the father is *not in him*."

What is the "world"? From the Bible, we see that it is the system of ideas and ways of living that are evil, against God, ruled by the Devil, and headed for Hell. The true Christians have been saved *from* it; they must refuse to *live* like it;

they must keep clean from it and remain forever *against* it. There is no such thing as a "worldly Christian." Paul said, "Because of the cross, the ways of this world are *dead* to me and I am *dead* to them." (Galatians 6:14).

Living like the world does not have to do with *things*. Worldly living is a heart-attitude. Worldly living is that which in spirit and feelings, the children of the world love, esteem, and enjoy; what has no reference to God, righteousness, or eternity; and everything that is spiritually against a dignified, committed, useful Christian character. It is a spirit of giving in to selfish ways of life. It means to copy the standards of lost people instead of living like Jesus. If you want to serve Him, you will not copy the fads and fashions of selfish society. You will take your marks from the Lord Jesus and His book.

THE IN-CROWD IS IN TROUBLE

It is hard to be *lonely*. Many kids today would rather *sell their souls* than to feel left out of the crowd. When you are young there is great pressure on you to "fit in." But if the crowd is *wrong*, fitting in with them will hurt God. The youth scene shows constant change from idea to idea, a series of searches to bring kids together with God. About the only thing most of these ideas do have in common is the fact that they are all things kids can do together. Most ideas become merely that which is hip at the time, and are not seriously practiced.

The need to belong can be a real addiction. It can be just as strong a temptation as drugs or sex. Some kids would rather mix in with a rotten crowd than walk out if it meant standing alone to do right. And Satan knows this. If he can make even *Jesus* just another fad — if he can make the Gospel just a cover to

HE'S BEEN FOUR HOURS WITHOUT HIS FRIENDS. I THINK IT'S WITHDRAWAL

bring people together without a need to change their hearts — he will succeed in using the Gospel *against* the Gospel. It is possible for kids to unite around "Jesus," not because they really believe in, or obey His word, but because His name is bringing people together. And this will sell Him out like Judas did again. He will not be presented as He *is*, a threat to wicked living and the hang-loose trip, but just as the next step in an evolving drive to get it all together.

Resist the temptation to be "in" all the time. *The way of the crowd is usually the wrong way.* The Christian has been called to go against the crowd. The world is against God. If we want to follow the Lord Jesus, we must go against the world's ways and attitudes. Remember: If selfish people are all *for* it, then God is usually *against* it.

Some Christians follow the world's ways without knowing it. Whatever new thing is in they take pains to show that Jesus says the same thing. If drugs are in, it is easy to say, "Jesus will get you high too." We do need to speak in words that the world will understand, that lost people can grasp. But we are not free to put Jesus and His standards into someone else's mold. He is the standard by Whom all lives must be reassured. Serving Jesus is not just a way of feeling good or leaving problems behind. Don't tie the Eternal God to changing fads of the world. He never changes. He is the same always.

HABITS

Unsaved people ought to EXPECT Christians to be different. We are strangers to this world. We are to be so different in our conduct, speech, and motives that we generate respect and awe for our walk with God. We are to live in purity and holiness, loving the things God loves, and hating the things God hates. We are, by our lives,

DON'T TALK TO ME I'M ALREADY A CHRISTIAN

to awaken the conscience of men and women who ought not to look at us and say to themselves: "We can't be *too* wrong, or these Christians wouldn't put up with what we are doing, or find pleasure in the same things we do. There is not really so much difference between us and them, except that they are religious and we are not." We should enjoy different things, because "if any man be in Christ, he is a new creation; old things are passed away; all things are become new." *Madam Guyon,* that saintly woman of God said:

> "I bade farewell forever to assemblies which I had visited, to plays, diversions and dancing, unprofitable walks, and parties of pleasure. The amusements and pleasures, so much prized and esteemed by the world, now appeared to me dull and insipid — so much so, that I wondered how I ever could have enjoyed them."

Let's look at some of the more common habits of the world:

SMOKING

Smoking is still an issue with some Christians. We need to ask ourselves some serious questions about it if it is a habit we have indulged in. (a) My body is the TEMPLE of the Holy Spirit. Does a cigarette make my body better fitted to be His dwelling-place? (b) *WHY* am I smoking? How did I begin? Was it to impress a crowd; or to please a friend; or to feel "in" at the time; or because I was tense and worried? Are these reasons good enough for me to continue doing it?

Don Lonie said, "A guy takes up smoking to prove that he is a man; and ten years later he tries to give it up to prove the same thing." Now, when faced with discussions on this subject, some people just refuse to look at it. There was a man who read that cigarette smoking causes cancer, so he gave up *reading*. But there are good reasons why Christians should not smoke. Here are a few:

(A) A Christian tells the world that he finds rest, relaxation, and stimulus in his experience in *Christ* and in the disciplines of the Gospel. Thus, smoking is a NEEDLESS habit. No Christian ought to need a noxious stimulant to function.

(B) Smoking is a *DANGEROUS* habit. Many toxins in cigarette smoke are unquestionably related to dangerous diseases including heart, lung, and respiratory disease and failure, as well as cancer. Our bodies don't belong to ourselves, but to God.

(C) It is an *UNFAIR* HABIT. It forces all others who share a room with a smoker to inhale the same, or even secondhand stale smoke. In buses, planes, trains, and other public places, it forces a nonsmoker to participate in his bad habit.

(D) It is a *FILTHY* habit. Smoking is a process by which a toasted and dried weed is burned in a paper cylinder or other receptacle to create inhaled smoke, leaving ash and the partially burned remains of the weed. The smoke stains the teeth, corrupts the breath, marks the fingers, pollutes the air, and fouls the clothing — not only of the smoker, but all in his reach. The ashes and butts have a ministry of their own; they can pile up in an unsightly mess, burn tables, carpets, and sometimes beds with the smoker still sleeping in them (including the room and house around him). And how can this habit be justified by a *Christian* who claims to represent the Son of God to the world?

(E) It is a *WASTE* of *time,* of *money*, and of *health* — GOD'S time, GOD'S money, and the health of a body that belongs to GOD. C. G. Finney tells of a man who was battling with the smoking habit who saw it one day in the light of the cross. He said to himself, "Did Christ *die* to purchase this vile indulgence for me?" And he was instantly delivered from it. Can a Christian justify the spending of God's money on a habit that is neither edifying, ennobling, or useful, and even worse than this, actually *harmful*?

(F) It is a *stumbling block*. In most societies, liquor, gambling, and cigarettes are indelibly associated with the spirit of a secular society, of external signs of addiction to pleasure and the stimulation of jaded senses. Here you must ask too, "Am I, by my actions, causing a brother to stumble? Is my action bewildering or confusing him, giving him encouragement to sin or setting him a bad example? Do I want those I lead to Christ to be like me also (because if I still smoke, so will they)? I cannot urge them to give up any harmful habit when I myself hold on to my own pet one."

(G) There is a better case for *liquor* in the Bible than there is for cigarettes; and the liquor case is *small indeed*. Some wines can be drunk in moderation for medicinal reasons with a measure of benefit to the system. This is not true of smoking. *Every* cigarette is harmful. No cigarette is beneficial. And the next one simply adds to the danger of the last. The Bible has a number of verses on smoking or smoke, although the habit itself was not invented in Bible days. It is used as a metaphor for *slothfulness* (Proverbs 10:26); a simile for those that *aggrevate God* (Isaiah 65:5); for *death* (Psalms 102:3), *punishment* (Psalms 68:2), *hell* (Revelation 14:1; 19:3); and the *judgment of the system* of the world (Revelation 18:18). And what case can a "smoking Christian" build against smoking grass or marijuana — against shooting drugs, against dropping acid; or, for that matter, what case can he build to convince someone who wants to follow Jesus that he should pray for deliverance from any *binding habit at all* which is simply misused slavery to stimulation? The principle in each is the same; they are *habits that bind*, which are harmful to us. D. L. Moody said that a man came to him and said he "wanted a scripture that said a Christian should stop smoking." Moody said he couldn't give him one, but that he *could* give him one that said a person should go on smoking. He gave him Revelation 22:11: ". . . and he which is filthy, let him be *filthy still.*" No Christian should smoke. Smoke is what happens when the flame doesn't burn hot enough. People who smoke who call themselves Christians need to get nearer the fire.

DRUGS

Drugs are not a new problem. Man has used them for thousands of years. The East has always known and used drugs as a part of some of their religious rituals. People have always known about plants or chemicals that would do things to their feelings or thoughts. What *is* new is that people all over the world have turned to drugs trying to find *answers* to problems science has found too big to handle. What has happened to God's world because of the drug explosion?

The drug abuse "mushroom" has had terrible results. Millions of people have become addicts and cannot give up their drug habits. Multiplied thousands die from bad chemicals or overdoses, and thousands more from bad trips that led to suicide or accidental death. The drug scene began with people smoking grass and throwing kisses and flowers. The apparent beauty *ended* in a few short months, ended with people burning each other, throwing rocks, bottles, and knives. The pleasures of sin are only for a short season; the end of that season is all too often insanity, disease, and death.

But the greatest problem with mind drugs is not the "bad" trips. It is the *"good"* ones that cannot be brought down into real life. Here is a young man who goes up with a cap of acid. In his trip, he feels artistic; colors and texture seem alive in his head and fingers. He grabs a brush and paints, covering the can-vas with what looks like

a perfect masterpiece. He has never done anything that looked so beautiful. Many hours later, he comes *down*. He sees his painting as it really is without a chemical to color his mind. It is then that shock hits him; the empty promise of the drug vision shows itself for what it really is. His picture is nothing but a scribbled scrawl of smeared paint. His masterpiece was an illusion. It was all in his mind, and is now gone, gone forever.

This is what really hurts in the drug scene. The "expanded mind" is so unreal and unnatural. Colors and scenes come from chemicals. Your world is only pretty when your mind is the slave of a drug. When it wears off — there's the *same old world*, same old problems. You are still the *same* person as before; sometimes, you are even worse off. Often it takes bigger doses to get the same levels of experience the next time. Nothing is different. Your guilt, loneliness, and emptiness are *still there* waiting for you.

How different it is with Jesus! "Heaven above is softer blue; earth beneath is sweeter green; something lives in every hue, Christless eyes have never seen. Someone wrote who knew the reality of God's Word and God's Son. The whole earth is beautiful when you know the One Who made it. Your soul becomes clear; your inner, spiritual eyes open to see the loveliness of His creation. The loneliness is gone. The world no longer seems empty or meaningless. Listen to what one young man said about God's power by the Holy Spirit in his life:

> ". . . He gave me such a blessing as I have never dreamed a man can have this side of heaven. It was an unutterable revelation. It was a heaven of love that came into my heart. My soul melted like wax before the fire. I sobbed and sobbed. I loathed myself that I had ever sinned against Him, or lived for myself and not for His glory. Every ambition for self was now gone. The pure flame of love had burned it like a blazing fire would burn a moth.

I walked out over Boston Commons before breakfast, weeping, and praising God. Oh, how I loved! In that hour, I knew Jesus and loved Him till it seemed my heart would break with love. I was filled with love for all His little creatures. I saw the little sparrows chattering; I loved them. I saw a little worm wriggling across my path; I stepped over it. I didn't want to hurt any living thing. I loved the dogs; I loved the horses; I loved the little urchins in the streets, I loved the strangers who hurried past me — *I loved the whole world!*"

Samuel Logan Brengle, *Portrait of a Prophet*

No one who has ever lived, and loved the Bible God ever needs drugs again. His joy is direct, immediate, real. And the Bible *has* something to say about drugs. It mentions *four* powerful ones, two which are stronger than L.S.D. They are *wormwood, hemlock, gall,* and *myrrh.* (Amos 6:12, Deuteronomy 28:18; 32:32) On a drug strength scale,  *hemlock* comes right after alcohol and caffeine; *gall* comes after nicotine, pot, peyote, locoweed, nembutal, phenobarbital, and seconal; then after L.S.D. and opium, comes the last two, *wormwood* and *myrrh.* Heroin, and speed follow after these. *None* are ever used in the Bible to induce visions of the Biblical God, nor did any prophet of God ever use drugs to speak or listen to Him in the Scriptures. Anything that takes away the conscious control of our mind or feelings is a sin against our souls. No one has the right to put their bodies and spirits at the mercy of chemicals which open the door of their lives to the dangerous spirit world. No true Christian uses drugs. It is worthwhile to note that Jesus Himself was only offered a drug mixture *once* in His life — when, in dying pain, He could have had the best excuse for it — and He *REFUSED* it. (Mark 15:23; Psalms 69:21; Matthew 27:34)

WHAT TO SAY WHEN YOU STAND UP FOR RIGHT

How do you refuse to take part in an activity without putting down the person who asks you? There are a few things you should remember:

(A) Most times, you can simply *smile* and *refuse* without going any deeper into it. If you are offered a smoke, drugs, or drink, simply say, "No thanks" — either "No, thanks. I don't drink"; or "No thanks I don't smoke,"; or "No thanks, I don't use drugs." Say it simply, sweetly, with a smile. Don't put them down by looks or words in any way.

(B) If they ask you *why not*, or press you, just give a straight short *testimony* for the Lord. That will almost always finish off all offers; and secretly, they may admire you for your stand. Just say, "Well, to tell you the truth, I've given my life to Jesus, and He owns my body. I don't need (drugs, cigarettes, drink)." Or something like, "I know you may think this is a little strange, but I've given my life to the Lord Jesus and things like that don't matter to me anymore. To do this would violate my agreement with Him. I hope you will understand."

(C) If you want to lead into a witness, then use some of these "mystery" replies:

DRINK: "No thanks. I never touch the stuff now since I came across the drink they call 'Living Water.' Since I tasted that, I've never wanted any other drink again."

DRUGS: "No, thanks. I found something that is greater than the ultimate trip; and it never wears off. Once you start on it, you never want to use anything else."

OTHERS: "No, thanks! I can't do it . . . I'm dead!."
(Romans 6:2, 3, 6, 8, 11)

(D) For non-Christian guys who want to take you girls out on a date: "I'm honored by your invitation, but I'm afraid I can't accept." If he says, "Why not?" Then say, "I've given my life to Jesus and have decided that the guys I date must love Him more, if not the same as I do." If he says, "How will you know that's true if you don't go out with me?" Say, "I'd be happy to have you come and meet some of my friends so that we could talk about it." Then bring him to a meeting.

(E) If you girls have been going with a guy who is bad for you, and you want to break up with him, use, "I'm sorry I won't be able to go with you anymore. I'm married." If you have just become a Christian, Jesus is your spiritual Husband. (Isaiah 54:5; Ephesians 5:23)

REMEMBER: The secret of standing up for right is to be *POSITIVE* in your testimony. Suggest *alternatives* if you are invited some place that will compromise your life. For example: "I wouldn't like to go there, but how about us going _____ instead?" If you still get pressed, even after you have refused once and given your testimony, then you have one further step. Tell them, "You don't understand. I can't do this because I would *hurt God* if I did. He means more to me than anyone else in the world. It would be wrong and selfish for me to do this. I just plain can't do it."

XIII

KITCHEN: The Word Of God

Aha! — that very important room, the kitchen! Here is where your meals are prepared; here is where you serve up "soul food" for your all-important "inner man" of the spirit. Many failures in the Christian life come about by spiritual starvation. How's *your* eating?

"Man shall not live by bread alone, but by EVERY WORD that comes from the mouth of God." Jesus said it, and He meant it. Your Bible is the Greatest Book in the world. It is a manual of miracles. It is a Book *from* God *about* God; written BY His men about how to *be* His men and women. It is the story of His love for people. Its central figure is the *Lord Jesus*, The Messiah, God in the robe of a man. It is the record of His origin, birth, life, death, and resurrection. Its message is stranger than science fiction: The God who spun worlds into space has visited our earth to show us the way to heaven, and we may join a Love-Kingdom in His very own forever family. The Bible is no ordinary book; it is strangely different because it was written by men who listened to the voice of God. The words they wrote were more than human. They live like fire for each new Christian generation. In the power of the Holy Spirit, they are as fresh as the wind and rain on a mountain.

The Bible is not just a book of *history*, although its records have been clearly upheld by modern archeology. It is not a book of *poetry*, although it has inspired countless songs and poems through the centuries. It is not an *adventure story*, although few novels have matched the sheer drama of its pages. It is not a book on *ethics* or morals, yet civilization's finest and fairest laws have been forged from it. It is not a *textbook*; but it still amazes scientists and scholars from fields as widely different as sociology, medicine, and nuclear physics. The Bible is the unique revelation of man's problems and God's *answers*: The Good News of the love-revolution begun by the Father, given by the Son, and operated by the Holy Spirit. Yet *why* do so many people not understand or love it?

OPERATION DISCOVERY

It was just a letter you found lying on the ground. Curiosity got the better of you, so you opened it up and began to read. No, you didn't know  who wrote it, nor to whom it was written, but you understood the words and knew what it was talking about. Yet, it didn't seem to mean very much to you. Now why didn't you REALLY understand the letter? You knew the language. You understood the words. You could read the writing. Your problem? You didn't *know the writer*, and it *wasn't written* to you. The letter's message was as good as sealed or coded. The BIBLE is just like that. If you are not a real Christian, a man or woman who has given yourself to the Lord Jesus as your Saviour and Master, the Bible will be largely a sealed book. You don't know the Author; it doesn't speak much to you. When you get on REAL speaking terms with God, it will start to add up. Here's OPERATION DISCOVERY: KNOWING THE AUTHOR. If you don't really know Him now, why not begin? It is not enough to know ABOUT Him; you must KNOW HIM. When you are truly God's child, there is a world of adventure and discovery waiting for you in God's Word.

The first step in understanding the Bible is to begin to *READ IT*. Christians are people of His Book. There is no way to follow Jesus without also knowing and loving the Book He gave us. It is no accident that both Jesus and the Bible are called "The *Word of God*." (John 11:1; Revelation 19:3; Isaiah 8:20) Both are Divine. Both speak with power and authority. Both are fully true and trustworthy. The world needs Someone to know and Something to study. God gave us both a Book and His Son. We must obey both. We do not *love* Jesus more than we really love His Word. We do not *obey* Jesus more than we obey His Word. We do not *KNOW* God any more than we want to know His Word. Now, how much DO you read the Bible?

If you read only about FIVE MINUTES A DAY, you can finish it easily in less than a year. You can read the whole Bible through ALOUD in about seventy hours and forty minutes! The Old Testament read this way would take about fifty-two hours and twenty minutes; the New, would take eighteen hours, twenty minutes. If you were willing to spend *eight hours* a day on some holiday period, you could finish it in just *nine* days!

Reading by chapters takes you through the *whole Bible* in *eighteen* weeks at the rate of *ten a day*. That is *four* in the morning, *two* at lunch-time, and *four* more at night. The Old Testament read in this manner takes only fourteen weeks, the New Testament, twenty-six days. If you wanted to read just through the four *Gospels* (Matthew, Mark, Luke, John) together with Acts, you could read them in twelve days; all the rest of the books of the New Testament in another 15 days. Now, of course you may not want to do all of this; but how much of God's Book have you REALLY read? Jesus did *not* say, "You shall know the truth and the truth shall set you free." He said, "IF YOU CONTINUE IN MY WORD you are My disciple indeed; AND you shall know the truth, and the truth shall set you free." (John 8:32)

HOW TO READ THE BIBLE

Ask the *Holy Spirit* to help you understand what you read. Take colored pencils (ballpoints will slowly go right through the pages of most Bibles and ruin them) and MARK the verses that God speaks to you by. There are a few simple things to remember when you read the Bible. Keep them in mind, and you will not get funny ideas from the Devil or from people who don't know either the Scriptures or the power of God:

(1) *Read everything in the light of WHERE YOU FIND IT.* Don't pull bits out here and there and try to make them say something they don't really say at all in the place where they properly belong. Compare verses with other verses. (If some people read "Little Red Riding Hood" or "The Three Bears" the way they read the Bible,  they wouldn't understand those books either.) Be sure you have read *all* that you can find in the Bible on a subject before you teach others about it. God says those who teach from His Word have a solemn charge before Him to be right. (James 3:1-2; I Peter 4:10-11)

(2) *God's Book means EXACTLY WHAT IT SAYS.* Once you know what He is saying, take it EXACTLY AS IT IS. The only time you should think a verse is symbolic is when all verses around it clearly show that God wants it that way. Use *big* passages to help you understand the *little* ones; verses which *detail* things to help you understand other sections which are more general; and the ones where the writer is explaining carefully and factually to help you grasp others where the writer is just talking about what he feels or is enjoying in God.

(3) If some verses don't seem to fit, don't *force* them together. You just don't see the whole picture yet. Have you

ever done a jig saw puzzle? As you found bits that fit together, the whole picture became clearer. This is the way to read the Bible. Don't try to get it all at once. Just read in faith, believing that God will show you more as you read more.

USING BIBLE STUDY HELPS

(1) *A good CONCORDANCE:* This is a sort of "Bible Index." It is used like a dictionary when you are trying to find out where a verse appears in the Bible. You could, of course, read the whole Bible through carefully until you come across it. The other way is to use a concordance. If you can remember one word in the verse, just look up that word in the concordance (it lists all the words in the Bible in alphabetical order). When you find the list of words with your word in it, go through it until you come to the verse you want.

Of course, you can use a concordance for many other things. Use it for a Bible study on what God says about a topic. Some concordances give you original Hebrew or Greek words besides showing you how to say that word in English. Some have a special section in the end that gives you those Hebrew and Greek words in a list, and shows you how many times they are translated as one English word or as another. This special index is called a LEXICON. You will find lexicons at the back of both *STRONGS* and *YOUNGS* concordances.

(2) *A reliable DICTIONARY.* Use a well-known type like *WEBSTER'S or OXFORD'S* revised. With this you can look up words you don't understand and get ideas out of others that may help you get more meaning out of Biblical words. You can also buy a *BIBLE DICTIONARY.* This is written specially for Bible study, like the *BIBLE ATLAS* and *BIBLE ENCYCLOPEDIA.* These are helpful tools, but are not absolutely necessary for most of the things God can teach you. Be careful with *commentaries.* They are books where people explain to you what they think the Bible says. They can help, but may become a crutch to you, giving you a ready-

made traditional answer which may not be the truth of God. Some are quite useless in many areas of study. STAY SIMPLE when you study the Bible. Make sure that most of your study is the BIBLE ITSELF.

(3) *OTHER TRANSLATIONS:* The well-loved *KING JAMES VERSION* often uses words which have since changed their meaning. Other versions may help you understand a hard passage. The Bible was written in Greek, Hebrew, and Aramaic. When it has to be put

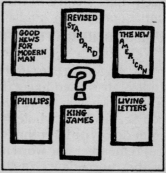

in our languages, men must try to translate it as best as they can. Sometimes they differ a little on what passages mean. Be careful of Bibles that have "interpretive notes" along with Bible verse. Some may be comments from fine, godly men; but you may start to rely on these to "explain" the "real meaning" of the Word of God without giving the Holy Spirit a chance to speak to you directly.

There is a difference between a TRANSLATION and a PARAPHRASE. A *translation* tries to give you the ACTUAL WORDS used by the original author in your own language, as closely as possible, even if the translator doesn't understand the full meaning of what he has carefully translated. Some translations other than the *King James Version* are the *Revised Standard, The New American Standard,* the *Moffat* and *Berkeley* versions, and the *Amplified Bible.* There are also translations of the New Testament like *"Good News For Modern Man."*

A PARAPHRASE is not as accurate as a translation. Here, the man who is translating takes a verse of the original language, and tries to put in his own words what HE thinks is the meaning of the original words. Sometimes he uses words that do not appear in the original languages at all. *Phillip's* and the *Living Bible* are like this. Use these for fresh looks at Bible verses, or for easy reading; but don't rely on them for accuracy.

MEMORIZING THE BIBLE

What if *all Bibles* were taken from the earth? There have been times before in history when people were killed or imprisoned for owning a copy in their home. Today there are people in parts of the world that cannot obtain a Bible, as they are an outlawed book in their country. How much of the Bible would YOU know if tomorrow this happened to you? Would you like to learn a lot, to store it in your heart? David said that this helped keep him from temptation, "Your Word have I hid in my heart, that I might not sin against You." (Psalms 119:11)

You can memorize WHOLE BOOKS of the Bible — learn them by heart! It sounds impossible, but it can be done. It will cost you just THREE THINGS:

(1) *DETERMINATION*

(2) *A DATE WITH GOD*

(3) *DISCIPLINE.*

Do you REALLY want to know the Bible? Memorize the Scriptures to make you strong and clear in your faith? That's STEP ONE: *Determination*. Grit your teeth! Are you willing to spend some TIME on this? Sacrifice (ouch!) at least half-an-hour a day? That's step TWO: a *DATE* with God. How far do you want to go in this? Just a little — or really with it? Take your courage in your bare hands for the next step THREE: *Discipline! WARNING:* The FIRST THREE WEEKS are going to be the toughest! It is going to cost you HALF-AN-HOUR each night — EVERY night. If you want to LEARN, you'll have to WORK. Now, don't do this so as to impress people, or you'll lose your reward. Do it for the Lord. Tell Him you want to serve Him better and are being obedient to His Word in studying to show yourself approved to Him. (II Timothy 2:15) Then begin this study plan:

Day 1: *READ* the first chapter you want to memorize over and over again so you know it well. Do this at least TWENTY MINUTES. Then make an OUTLINE of the entire chapter; chart up all the places, people, things, and ideas as they appear. You will need to make yourself a special STUDY BOOK. A well-bound, loose-leaf folder is the best, if your funds permit. Draw up your chart and work it out on a scrap of paper, then redraw it into your notebook. It should not take you too long, but it should be clear and simple.

Day 2: *REVIEW* the first outline and list *KEY WORDS, KEY VERSES.* Take out about ten verses that you feel are important and make a set of memory cards as shown in "STUDY." Begin to memorize these verses. Write them out in full, saying them aloud. Get the content of each one. Also write out each verse in order of appearance in your study notebook. Don't spend time on the other parts of the chapter which you feel are less important.

Day 3: *WRITE OUT* some *QUESTIONS* on this chapter. Go for at least a hundred on each chapter you are studying. Ask your questions in all possible ways: Spelling of words, the "who, why, what, where, when, and how" series, just as if you were going to be quizzed on it. Put all of these questions neatly in your study book.

Day 4: *STUDY* your written questions, and *REVIEW* your memorized verses. Quiz yourself on what you have read by your questions and your memory cards. Be strict; but if you don't remember something, mark it down.

Day 5: *RE-REVIEW* memory verses, and pick up important old material that you have passed over before. Look for things you missed previously and put them in.

Day 6: *POLISH* your chapter up and get ready for a quiz with a friend or relative. Then let them run through some of your questions with you and check your answers.

Day 7: *PRACTICE* your knowledge; for the best results, let someone else who is also memorizing ask you some of their questions, and then you ask them some of yours on the same chapter. It will not become a real part of you until you USE it with someone.

Go over your material CONSTANTLY. Read chapters in buses, standing in line, in your spare time. Read a WHOLE BOOK THROUGH in one sitting if possible. Find your best time for study; morning, evening, or night, and fix your time for memorization there. God gives us the best times to memorize His Word in Deuteronomy 6:7, "These words which I command you this day shall be in your heart . . . and you shall talk of them . . .

(a) ". . . When you *sit in your house* . . ." (resting in our homes, sitting for meals or study)

(b) ". . . When you *walk in the way* . . ." (traveling to and from work and school)

(c) ". . . When you *lie down* . . ." (before we go to sleep at night, just before lights out)

(d) ". . . When you *rise up* . . ." (first thing in the morning when you get ready for a new day).

MARCHING ORDERS

Your Bible study and memorization will probably whet your appetite to expand what you read every day into other parts of the Bible. Here are some ways you can get "marching orders" for the day from the Bible:

(1) *PRAY BEFORE YOU READ*, asking God to guide you. Then open the book at random, and just begin to read from there until a certain verse "gets" you. STOP right

there. THINK. What does it mean? What could the Lord be trying to say to you from this? What can you learn from it? Does it apply to you, or to your friends, or to your activities? Remember the reference, mark it in your Bible and memorize the verse.

(2) *EXTEND* your prayer time and WAIT quietly on God. Ask Him to direct you to a passage. Wait until a certain book, verse, or chapter comes to mind. Look it up and begin to read, looking for a verse that "lives" to you. Remember that God wants to speak to you and teach you from its pages. Open your heart. God has something JUST FOR YOU. Don't rush!

(3) *Read SYSTEMATICALLY*. Read two chapters of the Old Testament to one of the New, and you will finish both at about the same time. Don't get BOGGED with long lists of names, chronology tables, health and sacrificial laws, etc. They all are important and have a purpose, but if you reach a passage you can't understand after a moment's thought, LEAVE IT. God may open up your understanding to it later when you have grown more spiritually. There are many things in the Bible that still continue to puzzle the wisest minds. Even Peter said of some of Paul's writings: "As also in his epistles, speaking of these things; in which are some things hard to be understood . . ." (II Peter 3:16)

(4) *Take* up *a SPECIFIC STUDY*. A Biblical character, like Peter, or Moses, or Elijah; a Biblical word like "faith", or "love", or "repent." Use a concordance to look up linking words and thoughts and/or center-column references (little verses or letters and numbers in the margins of some Bibles that refer you to other Scriptures or give alternate meanings).

XIV

DRAWINGROOM: Witness

Every home must have a *drawingroom*, a place where you can introduce friends to each other. And *your* home must have a drawingroom; that is the place where the Holy Spirit will draw others to knowing and loving your great Friend. How is your witness?

THE TEENAGE TORCHES

"So you Christian teenager, I have set you as a watchman in your school campus; therefore you shall hear what I tell you and warn them from Me.

"When I say to the unsaved man or woman — 'Unsaved man or woman, you shall die in your sins' — and you do not SPEAK to tell the unsaved one, nor WARN him from his wicked way; that very same person will DIE IN HIS SIN — but HIS BLOOD WILL I REQUIRE AT YOUR HAND."

"Doorways to Discipleship" centers on one *urgent fact*: We MUST tell others of the same Lord Who changed our lives.

All of these sections have been discussed with you to help you to be the kind of person who can speak with power and success of the Lord Jesus to your school, your community, and to your world. This is the goal of this book on being a disciple of Jesus — to help you match your life in all areas to God's standards, so that the message you preach will be backed up by a life that radiates its truth.

"You are the light of the world," Jesus said. "A city that is set on a hill cannot be hid." If by the grace of God, you have begun to put into action some of this material, and your life for the first time has begun to really balance, for the first time, you also will have begun to experience the tremendous thrill of a life lived in total dedication to the claims of Christ. God bless you, friend; only eternity will show the effect of your sacrifice and consecration on the world.

" . . . Let no man despise your youth — but you be an EXAMPLE of the believers..." Paul said to Timothy. (I Timothy 4:2) You have been called to Jesus' side in His search-and-redeem mission; it is the hardest, costliest, but most rewarding job in the world — reclaiming from a world that has sold itself to the Devil, souls that belong  to God. Once you have begun, you will never taste a greater thrill. It will affect you on earth, and move all the host of heaven. It may be a lonely job as far as friends on earth are concerned. You will probably be laughed at, or scorned, or despised, but with Friend Jesus at your side you will never, never be completely misunderstood or lonely or afraid again.

"Teenage torches" — lights blazing for God as the world goes into the twilight of its darkest hour. Torches lit by the oil of the Holy Spirit and the flame of God's love. "So let your light shine before men, so that they may see your good works and glorify YOUR FATHER which is in heaven."

BEFORE YOU BEGIN:

(1) *It is not going to be easy.* Our battle is not with flesh and blood. Words alone will not change men. You will need supernatural power to pit your prayers against the dark spirit that blinds the minds and hearts of lost men and women. ". . . If our gospel be hid, it is hid to them that are lost: In whom the god of this world has blinded the minds of them which believe not, lest the light of the glorious Gospel of Christ, Who is the image of God should shine unto them." (2 Corinthians 4:3-4) ". . . Because when they knew God, they did not give Him glory as God, neither were they thankful; but became vain in their reasonings, and their foolish heart was darkened." (Romans 1:21)

(2) *Remember WHAT you are doing.* You are not trying to "make converts." *God* is the One who must do the work of changing people's lives. You have a simple story to tell — of what happened to *you*, and what can happen to *them*. And remember WHY you are going out to share; because God's heart is being broken by people who do not love or obey Him.

EVERYONE MUST KNOW THE GOOD NEWS

The Lord Jesus knew that *one* soul was worth more than all the world. Most of His time was spent just talking with people about how they stood with God. He did not write any books, although He could easily have been the world's greatest author. He didn't give out one tract. He never had a course on soul-winning. He never learned or taught even *one plan* on how to win souls. But the one thing He did do every day was to "seek and save that which was lost."

You don't have to "learn" to be a witness. You already *ARE* a witness. Each day the world sees by your words and deeds who REALLY means most to you in life. You always get across to people what you ACTUALLY are most interested in. Your actions, words, and even your attitudes tell the world who you love most. If I follow you around for a day, read the books you like to read, meet the friends you like to be with, go to the places you like to go and watch the things you spend your money on, watch what you laugh at most and get most excited about — I can tell in *that day* whether you are really a Christian or not.

If you call yourself a child of God, you already HAVE been witnessing. If you have claimed to belong to Jesus, but your *life* doesn't back up your words, people may have turned their backs on God because of you. The Lord Jesus said, "He that is not with Me is against Me; and he that gathers not with Me is scattering abroad."

To be a witness means to be REAL – absolutely *real*. God hates phonies. If you have any reason in wanting to witness, apart from a real concern and love for both God and for people, forget it. You will do more harm than good. Only love will win hardened street people, kids at your school, or people around your block. It means concern for the God Whose heart has been broken over the sinner and his sin. It means living a life of true giving, giving of strength and time and care. And this love is not just something you FEEL. It is something you Do and is measured directly by your sacrifices.

To be a witness means also *living like Jesus did.* Our world is filled with selfish people who *think* only of themselves, *care* only for themselves, and *live* only for themselves. Jesus' friends must be different. It will do you no good to go to unsaved people and say, "Don't look at *me* for an example. I'm filled with greed, lust, bitterness, and hate. My life is an awful mess. I just want you to look at Jesus." That sounds spiritual, but it is not. The sinner cannot SEE Jesus. He can only see YOU. And he has a perfect right to say, "But I can't *see* Jesus. I can only see you. And if He can't help you, what makes you think He can help me?"

To be a witness for Jesus, we must live so far above the world's standards and values that unbelievers will take notice and ask us what is the secret of our lives. We must live so that we can say with Paul, "Those things which you have both learned and received and SEEN IN ME, *do*; and the God of peace shall be with you." (Philippians 4:9) Men must be able to be followers of *us* and of the *Lord at the same time. (I Thessalonians 4:6) Everyone must know the good news. They will only know it if we live such a life of joy, faith, and love that we can say in the energy of God, "Be ye followers of me, even as I am of Christ." (I Corinthians 11:1) Remember this:*

"We are the only Bibles
This careless world will read.
We are the *sinner's* Gospel;
We are the *scoffer's* creed.
We are the Lord's last message,
Given in deed and word.
What if the type is *crooked?*
What if the print is *blurred?*"

OPERATION OUTREACH

Here is a pattern for reaching your unsaved friends with the Gospel. No plan or program will change people. Only the Holy Spirit can do that. But you must be wise when you win souls. Jesus was.

(1) *RAP:* Establish *CONTACT* with him or her. Are they your *friend?* Do they know that you are a friend to them, that you care about them as people, that you are interested in their lives, and their happiness? Here is where your LIFE will be all-important. No man or woman is going to buy your message unless it is packaged in a life that demonstrates it. Get a common *interest* point. Choose a young person in your sphere of influence.

(2) *CONTACT for the Gospel.* Bring that person, who is your friend, under the sound of the Gospel. Invite them out to meetings in your town where you know the Word of God will be presented in simplicity, in power, and in common language. Or introduce your friend to your other Christian friends and let him or her feel their love, acceptance, and warmth. Jesus said, "By this shall all men know that you are my disciples; if you have *love* one to another." The world will not believe in Jesus until it believes in our lives and our reality. That is why it is so important to have a clean and Christ-honoring life.

(3) *WAIT* for the "green light." Let *God* set up the opportunity to lead that person through to saving knowledge of Jesus. It will become the most natural thing in the world. Don't try to force an opening for the Holy Spirit. Just bring them into contact with the work of God and then wait, and pray, and watch for God's moment to open the conversation for Him. You can pray each day before you go to school or work that God will give you an opportunity to speak to someone that day about their soul. Then go through the day with your eyes open and wait for God to present the opportunity. This is the real thrill of witness; the adventure of working with God, the Holy Spirit, on a day-by-day search for hungry, lost people.

ABC'S OF OPERATION OUTREACH

A. APPROACH: To really get across your message, you must know and love your friend, and the interests he has along one or more of the basic four areas of your life:

PHYSICAL: The sport-loving, athletic.
MENTAL: The intellectual, studious.
SOCIAL: The party-goers, the ones who want to be "in" or popular.
SPIRITUAL: The "already-religous" — the hardest kind to reach.

B. *ATTITUDES.* A lot of fear in witness comes because we are afraid of what people will think of us when we present the Gospel. Here are the *five things* people can say when you speak to them about Jesus. Read them, and it will help you deal with fear. If someone reacts in one of those five ways, just chalk it down, "Oh well — number five!"

1. *ACCEPTANCE:* "I want to get saved." The person gets ready to give their life to God right there. This usually means that person has been dealt with by the Lord already. Check that they really *understand* what they are doing. *Suspect* quick decisions made without any signs of struggle, cost, or surrender; also be suspicious when there is no apparent change after prayer. And no decisions should be made while a person is high on drugs or stoned out of their mind on alcohol! Sometimes God can bring people down while they are high and really save them; but usually, it is best to either pray them down or wait until the drug wears off before you do any serious talking to them about Jesus.

2. *CURIOSITY:* A sign of awakened hunger or interest. Present as simply as possible God's claims on their life. Use love, smile at yourself now and then, but be in earnest and be firm. Ask QUESTIONS to make sure they understand what you are talking about. They will be looking at YOU during this time, trying to work out whether you are real or not. That is why it pays to be totally honest and really personal.

3. *HESITANCE:* "I have my doubts." Often this is a sign of sin being exposed. If they ask questions here that you feel are really only a sort of excuse, bring them kindly and gently back to their own personal responsibility. Now you can see why *"Doorways to Discipleship"* has encouraged you to STUDY to show your‑  self approved to God! You will need answers that *really* answer.

4. *INDIFFERENCE:* The worst kind. "So what?" The "hang-loose" trip has affected a lot of heads and hearts. That is why prayer is such an important part of witness. Only reality will cut through the mask of indifference. You show them that YOU care because God cares even if they don't. A firm and loving warning from the Word of God is your only tool here. Bob Harrington tells of flying on a plane with an unsaved businessman during a violent storm. The businessman shrugged off his witness. Bob pointed out the window and said, "Mister, what do you see?" The man looked. "A wing and two motors." "That's right," said the 'Chaplain of Bourbon Street,' "And if those two motors go, I'll have your soul for Christ before we hit the ground." Just a little later, as the plane bucked and jolted the man blurted out, "You're right. I need to get saved."

5. *REJECTION:* "Go hang it on your nose." Or nicer epithets. Show your grief and concern for them. Sometimes a warning from a concerned man or woman of God has spoken to a sinner months later when they have brushed close with Death, and came out on Christ's side.

C. *BEHAVIOR:* Paul's directions to Timothy tell us how to live as a witness before the world, "Let no man despise your youth; but be an example of the believers in word, in conversation, in charity, in spirit, in faith, and in purity." (I Timothy 4:12) *WORD* — What you *SAY* — your *message*. Don't preach a Gospel that Jesus cannot justify. Be sure you share salvation on God's terms and in His way. Lay it out like Jesus did. *CONVERSATION* or *LIFE* — what you *DO* — your *actions*. God's plan is to incarnate His Son again in the lives of His people, and put Him on display through them to the world. You must be a living example of what Jesus is like to the man who doesn't know Him. *CHARITY* — or *LOVE* — why you DO it — your *motives*. If you have let God search out your heart and flood your life with real care and compassion, you will have pure motives. *SPIRIT – WHEN* you witness — the ability to be led and directed by the Holy Spirit. You cannot witness effectively without knowing His power in a daily, direct way. *FAITH – HOW* you do it — the ability to HOLD ON in prayer and patience, believing that with God all things are possible, no matter how much a man or woman has gone into sin. *PURITY — WHERE* you witness — the power of a pure heart can keep you straight inside when your mission-field is sold out to sin; the ability of inside insulation, not isolation. The Christian ought to be able to go into Hell and not come out with the smell of burning on his clothes. He has given in to God, and he will not give in to the sin of the places in which he speaks for His Lord. Your approach must be:

POSITIVE: (Not a lot of DON'TS; deal with the HEART)

POINTED: (AIM at one specific person — deal directly)

PRACTICAL: (Life-experiences to prove Jesus really meets needs)

D. *BARRIERS:* When truth comes home to the heart, sinners throw up their defenses. Get ready for one of these four to come your way when you witness, or a combination of them:

(1) *MENTAL: Argument.* "The Bible is just another religious book." "I can't believe that a God of love would let the world live in war." "I'm just as good as you are!" *Don't argue back!* Answer by *raising a further question*, like "What evidence do you have for that?", or by further defining what you have just said. Answer with FACTS, don't raise your voice, don't get angry, sarcastic, and don't ridicule. If you know his argument is just an excuse, smile and point that out to him. Stick to the basics; keep pressing them home; and don't get sidetracked by "smoke screens." If you don't know an answer, be honest and say, "I don't know. But if you really want to know, I'll try to find out for you." Then go and do some more Bible study.

(2) *PHYSICAL:* You may be physically struck in your witness for Jesus. It is rare in most "Gospelized" countries; but it could happen. In this case, you are under direct command to "resist not" evil. (Matthew 5:38-48) You may not be able to control

your *feelings* of hurt or anger if this happens, but you can cry out inside for help to make the right choice and not strike back. This is showing true love, and "turning the other cheek."

(3) *SOCIAL: Avoiding* you. One of the most common barriers. Sinners start to steer clear of you if your witness hits home. Don't "trail them around" if this is happening; just "happen to be there at key times. If your witness has been loving and kind, they are not really trying to hide from *you* but from God. Get across to them your love and the fact that you are praying for them.

(4) *SPIRITUAL:* "Assuring" you that they are already saved; they belong to a "good church"; they have their "own religion," thank you very much! Clarify the "religious sinner's" stand by asking them about the events which led up to their giving their lives to God. Point out that the marks of a true Christian are a genuine devotion to the Lord Jesus and the love of God which marks an unselfish life. Often religious fronts are markedly like real faith; but if you know your Bible and know how to pray, you will be able to pick the fine differences and demonstrate what the real thing looks like.

E. DEALING WITH BARRIERS

CONSISTENCY: The ability to be the SAME all the time. You must develop proper responses to these barriers that come up:

PHYSICAL: Stephen beat this barrier — "Lord, I'm not my own, I've been bought with a price." To forgive, return good for evil, be reviled and not revile again are tests of true faith. Jesus suffered for us; it is a privilege to follow in His steps. (I Peter 2:21)

MENTAL: "Lord, I don't know all the answers, but I know You!" Deal with questions honestly and use the ones you *can't* handle as basics for your Bible study to help you grow.

SOCIAL: "Lord, they might shun ME, but they can't avoid YOU!" You are NOT the only person that God can use to speak to someone. Pray, and ask God for other witnesses for your friend.

SPIRITUAL: The Christian life REALLY LIVED shows up the difference! True faith differs from false faith as chalk is different from cheese. God says, "Love not the world, neither the things that are in the world. If any man love the world, the love of the Father is not in him. For all that is in the world, the lust of the flesh, and the lust of the eyes, and the pride of life is not of the Father, but of the world. And the world passes away and the lust of it; but he that does the will of God abides forever." (I John 2:15-17)

CONVICTION: No two young people experience it in quite the same way. The Bible word meaning "convict" is a legal word; it means to "sum up the evidence and present it before the mind" much as a lawyer would do before a judge and jury. It is translated as "convince" in John 16:8, or "reprove." To see conviction take place, we must have three things:

(1) The *WORD OF GOD* rightly applied to the conscience. God has promised only to honor His Word, not our own ideas or words. There will be no real conviction without it.

(2) The *WITNESS* of our own life. The Bible says, "Little children, let us not love in word, neither in tongue; but in deed and in truth." (I John 3:18)

(3) The Holy Spirit. Conviction comes when a person really SEES their selfish way of life. To do this, and to make sin real, is the task of the Holy Spirit. It may help to ask a person, "You ask God to show you how much you have hurt Him. Ask Him to bring to mind the things you have done to hurt yourself, others, and God."

DECLARATION of the Gospel: Bring your friend under the sound of the Gospel. If he or she wants to give their lives to Jesus, use **HOW TO BE SAVED** (p. 238). You must get across man's problem, God's solution, His conditions, and our responsibilities.

DECISION: The big moment. A true decision for Christ must involve the *MIND:* Knowing the facts and the *FEELINGS*: There is emotion in the love and in sorrow over sin; and the *WILL*: Faith leads to a committal of will to the person and work of the Lord Jesus. The decision is just the *beginning* of being a disciple of Christ. Being reborn is the *first* step to life.

XV

CLOSET: Prayer

Here, in this little room, is one of the key rooms in your house. It is very tiny, this closet we call "PRAYER". But it is the secret of communion with God.

"More things are wrought by PRAYER than this world dreams of; wherefore, let thy voice rise like a fountain both day and night."

Prayer is the vast, little known, and little-explored power which moves the arm of God, which shakes nations, blinds Hell, and accomplishes the impossible. Here's how you can really pray — and see miracles happen!

One of the most exciting rediscoveries of recent years was Rosalind Rinker's study of the *naturalness* of prayer. It is not a song, not a chant or repetition, but a *talk* between you and God. "Prayer is the *conversation* between two people who love each other." Here's some of her simple steps to revolutionize your prayer life:

(1) *Don't PRETEND with God.* Tell Him exactly what you think and feel. If there is sin in your life, admit it honestly,

just as it is, just as you know in your heart of hearts. Remember HE KNOWS; but it will help you be honest. He knows your heart.

(2) *Be NATURAL.* Don't try to force yourself to speak in a funny way. Remember, as well as being your Lord and Master, He is also your Father and Friend. The Bible does not tell us a particular set of words to say, but rather an attitude, one of reverence, thankfulness, adoration, praise, and love. Don't use God's Name as a punctuation mark: "Oh Father, I thank you, Father, that You, Father, can hear, Father . . ." Better to say nothing for a while than to push on mindlessly and use words just to fill in space.

(3) *Don't TALK TOO MUCH!* What would you think of a friend who phoned you, poured out a list of things he wanted, asked for a large number of favors, tacked on a quick word of thanks for things you had done in the past, and then HUNG UP, before you could say a word? Some prayer is like that! Take time to LISTEN to God, to let Him speak to your heart and to your mind. Learn to WAIT on Him.

HELLO LORD, PLEASE BLESS MY FAMILY AND BLESS ME. PLEASE GIVE ME A NEW CAR, A BETTER JOB, MORE MONEY, A NEW T.V., A PRETTY GIRL-FRIEND AND I'LL BE SURE TO THANK YOU FOR IT. AMEN.

(4) *Pray SPECIFICALLY.* What's the use of asking God to "bless the world and all the people in it?" How would you know if He did? If you want to see your prayers answered, why not PRAY for specific things? "Faith in a prayer-answering God makes a prayer-loving Christian." Make definite, faith-sized requests. Pray only for things which you can really *believe* God for. When you have seen those prayers answered, take another larger faith-sized "bite." This is the way to help you grow both in faith and prayer.

(5) *Pray ALWAYS.* This sounds like an impossibility, but it really means to always be in an ATTITUDE of prayer. It means to never get in a place where you can't pray readily and easily. If you have to "change gears" down inside, then

you are in the wrong place with God. Praying-always Christians live in miracles, and know real joy and guidance. You don't have to say LONG prayers — Peter's prayer wasn't! (Mark 14:30) You don't have to take a particular POSITION — God isn't so concerned about your BODY kneeling as He is about your HEART kneeling. You can pray at a school desk, on a playing field, walking along the road, or driving a car. You don't even have to CLOSE YOUR EYES. This helps keep your mind on God, of course, but with a little practice you can often pray without it. Jesus often "lifted up His eyes to Heaven" to pray. Praying with your eyes open is essential when you are counseling someone, and you need the Lord to guide you, or produce conviction of sin.

(6) *How about just THANKING Him?* Too often our prayers are just "request sessions!" What would you think of a "friend" who only asked you for things all the time! How much would you think that friend really cared for you? Should it be any different with your Heavenly Father? Why not spend a good TEN MINUTES just thanking God?

(7) Fight the temptation to *RUSH through* or *MISS OUT* a prayer-time. Realize it is an ATTACK on your spiritual life. If Satan can block our praying, he can ruin our effectiveness.

> "Satan *laughs* at the words we say;
> Smiles at our efforts from day to day.
> But he trembles when he sees,
> The weakest saint upon his knees."

Now here is a helpful thing to think about in prayer. PRAYER has been described as our "life breath", as our "weapon", as our "communication link" with Heaven; and many other things. But here is something that will help you more than anything. Prayer is WORK, spiritual WORK. It is *not* easy; it takes *discipline* and determination. But it is just as necessary as sermon preparation, Bible study, or any of the other Christian things you want to do. Of course, no one can *see* you pray, while a lot of people can hear your sermons or listen to your Christian witness. But when you pray, GOD SEES and so does the Devil. When you pray, you get a reputation in Hell. Prayer pits spiritual strength against the rulers of darkness and wickedness in high places who blind men's eyes to the light of God's truth. A. W. Tozer says, "Satan has no fear of LIGHT as long as he can prevent a victim from having SIGHT." Where as the WORD of God gives LIGHT, PRAYER helps lift the blinds of people's minds and give them SIGHT to see Jesus.

If *wandering thoughts* come drifting into your mind during prayer, PRAY about them. Your biggest battles will come when you are tired or sleepy — try to plan prayer sessions so that you will be fresh when you begin. Remember: PRAYER IS WORK. But it is the holiest and highest work we can do in the Kingdom of God.

(8) *GROUP prayer* is different. You are talking over your problems WITH EACH OTHER and sharing them with the Lord. Try this next time: Put out a chair for the Lord. Keep it empty for Him; visualize Him sitting there listening to you as you talk with each other in your prayer circle. How would you speak to Him? How would you speak to each other? He says, "Where two or three are gathered together IN MY NAME *there I am* in the midst." (Matthew 18:20) Pray first that God will lay some prayer burden on your heart. Then share it with others in your circle, and all pray together over it until you feel God has it in His hands and is going to answer. Keep each prayer short and don't be full of words. *D. L. Moody* said, "I never pray longer than five minutes; but I never go more than five minutes without praying." It is not the LENGTH of your prayers, but their STRENGTH that counts with God.

HOW TO PRAY AND GET ANSWERS

Have you ever wondered why God doesn't seem to answer some prayers? Check *your* prayer-life for any one of these answer-blockers:

(1) *The WICKED prayer*. Prayer for something God has forbidden will not be answered. To pray, we must stay within God's promises and laws. If we get out of these, God will not hear our petitions. The Bible says, "You ask and you do not receive because you ask amiss that you may spend it on your own lusts." (James 4:3)

(2) *The UNFORGIVING prayer*. If you try to pray with bitterness in your heart, God *cannot* answer until you are willing to repent. The only time we can expect answers from God to prayer at all, is when we have forgiven all the wrongs others have done us, and have been forgiven all our own wrongs. "And when you stand praying, forgive, if you have anything against anyone; that your Father also which is in Heaven may forgive you your trespasses. But

if you do not forgive, neither will your Father which is in Heaven forgive your trespasses." (Mark 11:25-26)

(3) *The SELFISH prayer*. This is when we are only praying with our personal interests in mind, not God's glory. We are to pray "in the Name of Jesus." This means that we are to come to the Father as JESUS HIMSELF would have come. To come in the "name" of some country is to come with its best interests at heart, and with all its rights and powers represented in your request. To come to the Father and pray in Jesus' Name is to come with the best interests of God at heart, and to come representing the Lord Jesus. And Jesus did not live for Himself. He did not pray just so that He could be more happy, but that His Father and the whole of Heaven could be more happy.

(4) *The CLUELESS prayer*. Sometimes we do not understand what we are praying for, and we do not know enough of the Word of God to pray wisely. Paul asked God three times to take away his "thorn in the flesh," but the Lord had

left it there as a safeguard to protect His apostle from getting too proud of what God had done in his life. "For this thing I besought the Lord three times, that it might depart from me." And He said to me, "My grace is sufficient for you; for my strength is made perfect in weakness." (II Corinthians 12:7-9)

(5) *The SELF-RIGHTEOUS prayer.* Secretly comparing ourselves more favorably than others. This kind of prayer only bounces off the ceiling. We don't come to God on the basis of "how far" we have advanced in the Christian life. We only come on the basis of the cross and blood of Christ, only as people whom He has brought back from sin and death by His grace. "And He spoke this parable to certain people which trusted *in themselves* that they were righteous, and despised others; . . . the Pharisee stood and prayed thus WITH HIMSELF . . . God, I thank You that I am not as other men are, extortioners, unjust, adulterers, or even as this publican . . ." (Luke 18:9-14)

(6) *The DOUBTING Prayer (Faithless),* and the WORDY prayer (Falseness) are also some prayers that won't get answered. To pray and get answers, don't pray unless you will REALLY *BELIEVE* God will answer. And strip your prayer-life of all wordy, foolish talk just for the sake of hearing yourself speak, or that's all that will happen.

Pray in *JESUS' NAME*. It is not just a charm, or a nice, Christian way to end a prayer. It is our *AUTHORITY* that gives us a right to speak with a Holy God; it is a *SEAL* that ensures that all we pray for is in line with the will of God, and is for His final glory; and it has POWER over the Enemy and his evil hosts. We can command evil forces in that Name to release their holds!

CONDITIONS FOR EFFECTIVE PRAYER

God will answer our prayers when we are careful to meet His conditions. Catherine Booth of the Salvation Army gave these *three basic conditions* as the "golden links" by which prayer connects with Heaven's switchboard:

(1) *LIVING AND ABIDING UNION WITH CHRIST.* "If you abide in Me," Jesus said, "and My Words abide in you,

you shall ask what you will and it shall be done unto you."
(John 15:7)

(2) *SYSTEMATIC OBEDIENCE* to the teachings of the
WORD AND THE SPIRIT of God. "Beloved, if our heart
condemn us not, then we have confidence towards God.
And whatsoever we ask, we receive of Him, because we
keep His commandments and do those things which are
pleasing in His sight." (I John 3:21-22)

(3) *UNWAVERING FAITH* in the truthfulness and faith-
fulness of God. "But let him ask in faith, nothing
wavering; for he that wavers
is like a wave of the sea, driv-
en with the wind and tossed.
For let not that man think
that he shall receive anything
of the Lord." (James 1:6-7)

Mrs. Charles Cowman tells
a story of how a philosopher
pleased Alexander the
Great. When asked for
money, Alexander gave the philosopher commission to
receive from the royal treasury whatever he wanted. The
philosopher demanded, in his king's name, a sum of
£10,000! (About $30,000) The treasurer refused to grant it
until he had told the king. The king listened but said he was
delighted and wanted the money instantly paid. By the
greatness of his request, he showed the high idea he held of
Alexander's greatness, riches, and generosity. And "if
Alexander gave like a king, shall not Jehovah give like a
God?"

When we learn to *live* in these promises of the Bible, we
shall learn what it means to have our prayers answered.
"ALL THINGS, whatsoever you ask in prayer, BELIEV-
ING, you shall receive." *God's Word must be true;* and if your
experience does not match the promises, you know that
there is probably something wrong with your experience.
Examine yourself. Repent from all known sin. Then prove

Him in prayer, and you will know what it means to have power with God. You will know how to pray and get answers.

"Men always ought to pray and not faint." (Luke 18:1) That little "ought" is *emphatic*. It implies an obligation as high as heaven. JESUS said, "Men ought ALWAYS to pray," and added, "and NOT TO FAINT."

> "I confess I do not always FEEL like praying when, judging by my feelings there is no one listening to my prayer. And then these words have stirred me; I OUGHT always to pray; I OUGHT to pray; I SHOULD NOT GROW FAINT in praying." The farmer ploughs his field often when he does not FEEL like it, but he expects a crop for his labors. Now, if prayer is a form of work, and OUR LABOR IS NOT IN VAIN IN THE LORD, should we not pray regardless of feelings?" (Samuel Logan Brengle)

THE PRAYER OF POWER

As your prayer-life begins to deepen, you will discover some of the key principles on which power in prayer can be built. Here are a few of these for you to deepen your prayer-life and make it more effective for the Lord Jesus and His Kingdom:

(1) *FAITH:* It's important that we really BELIEVE God for what we are asking. If we are sure it is in His will, by His Word and by His Spirit, then we should be BOLD in faith. God *will* answer no matter how difficult or even impossible it may seem to us as humans. Jesus said: *"Have faith in God.* Truly I say to you, whosoever shall say to this mountain, Be taken up and be cast into the sea; and shall not doubt in his heart, but shall BELIEVE that what he says comes to pass, he shall have it. Therefore I say to you ALL things whatsoever you pray and ask for, BELIEVE that you HAVE RECEIVED THEM and you shall have them." (Mark 11:22-24; Matthew 21:21,22) "If you have faith ... nothing shall be impossible to you." (Matthew 17:20) "Let him ask IN FAITH, nothing doubting." (James 1:6)

(2) The *SPIRIT:* We need to ask the help of the Holy Spirit for direction in prayer. Often we do not know *how* we should pray, or *what* we should ask for — it is his gracious ministry to lead us into what we should ask from our Heavenly Father. Charles Finney says in his autobiography:

> "The Lord taught me, in those early days of my Christian experience, many very important truths in regard to the spirit of prayer . . . it came upon me in the sense of a burden that crushed my heart, the nature of which I could not understand at all; but with it came an intense desire to pray . . . I could not say much. I could only groan with groanings loud and deep . . . For a long time I tried to get my prayer before the Lord; but somehow, words could not express it."

"Likewise, the Spirit also helps our infirmities; for we know not what we should pray for as we ought: But the *Spirit Himself* makes intercession for us with groanings which cannot be uttered . . ." (Romans 8:26) ". . . I will pray with the spirit, and I will pray with the understanding also." (I Corinthians 14:15a)

(3) *The WORD:* One of the best ways of praying is to get a promise from the Bible, fulfill its conditions, and "remind" the Lord about it. God has promised to honor and back up his word — you can pray with confidence!

> "A spirit of importunity sometimes came upon me so that I would say to God that He had made a *promise* to answer prayer, and I could not, and *would* not be denied. I felt so *certain* that He would hear me, and that faithfulness to His promises, and to Himself, rendered it impossible that He should not

hear and answer, that frequently I found myself saying to Him . . . 'I hope Thou doest not think that I can be denied. I come with Thy faithful promises in hand, and I *cannot* be denied.' I cannot tell how absurd unbelief looked to me and how certain it was, in my mind, that God would answer prayer — those prayers that from day to day and from hour to hour I found myself offering in such agony and faith." (Charles Finney, Autobiography.)

"And this is the confidence that we have in Him, that if we ask anything according to His will, He hears us; and if we know that He hears us, whatsoever we ask, we know that we have the petitions that we desired of Him." (I John 5:14-15)

(4) *FASTING:* If you really want an answer from God, try FASTING. Prayer and fasting, in operation together, convinces ourselves and God that we really mean business. In a fast, we are giving up things we really need in order to give ourselves more to God and to prayer. Fasting intensifies our prayer lives. It enables us to concentrate wholly on the Lord Jesus. Try missing a meal or two and spending the time you normally would be eating in, in prayer. Sometimes God may lead you into fasting by taking away all your appetite for food before a big test or prayer-battle for someone else. When the disciples had failed to cast out a demon from a boy, Jesus said, "This kind can come forth by nothing, but by prayer and fasting." (Mark 9:29)

(5) If all else fails, try *TEARS!* It sometimes helps to get away somewhere where you can be all alone with God, where there will be no one around to disturb you or where you in turn will not disturb anyone. Go up to a forest, or on a lonely hill, or in an empty house, and lock yourself away with God. Learn to CRY to the Lord; to pour out your soul in earnest, desperate prayer; to really CRY out your needs in a holy shout to heaven. Do you really want to go through to God's throne in time of great need and agony? Then learn to cry. "The eyes of the Lord are upon the righteous, and His ears are open unto their cry . . . the righteous cry,

and the Lord hears, and delivers them out of all their troubles. The Lord is nigh to them that are of a broken heart . . ." (Psalms 34:15-18) "Who (Christ) in the days of His flesh, when He had offered up prayers and supplications with strong crying and tears . . . was heard in that He feared." (Hebrews 5:7)

(6) *INTERCESSION:* Pray for others. Put yourself in their place. When you pray for them, feel their problems and difficulties. A rule of intercession is this: Always PRAY WHEN GOD LAYS THAT PERSON OR GROUP ON YOUR HEART. Never be disobedient to the Voice of God. Carry them in prayer, until God lifts the burden from you. Intercession has been called "the highest and holiest ministry." It is the highest form of prayer, and must form the backbone of every real move of God in a nation. Catherine Booth said, "Prayer is agony of the soul — wrestling of the Spirit. You know how men and women deal with one another when they are in desperate earnestness for something to be done. That is prayer whether it be done to man or God; and when you get your heart influenced, melted, wrought up and burdened by the Holy Ghost for souls, you will have power; and you will never pray but that somebody will be convinced — some poor soul's dark eyes will be opened and spiritual life will commence." *(Conditions of Effectual Prayer – Godliness)* God moves when His people are moved.

XVI

GENERATOR: Power

Down in this room is the hub of all the light and warmth and power of your home. Listen, and you can hear the quiet sound that tells you energy is filling the rooms. This is the one room that supports the rest of your house; let's go down and see if your generator is going the way God plans it.

YOU, GOD AND GUIDANCE

From the beginning of creation, when He flung the stars into the trackless hollow of space, God *has had a purpose for you* as a tiny part of His vast purpose for mankind. To know and follow God's purpose for our lives brings the joy and radiance of a Christ-guided life. Here's HOW — if you are willing!

(1) *Be sure you are FILLED WITH THE SPIRIT OF GOD.* Honestly, without this, you will never make it. To know the power of the Holy Spirit and to be sensitive to His voice is the difference between defeat and victory, failure and success, direction and aimlessness. There is a *PRICE* — God wants you empty of *self* and *sin*. HE is always ready to fill your heart — but you are not! (Luke 11:13) Be HONEST

with yourself and with Him. Be EARNEST. Confess your sin, ask His forgiveness. Then, just as you asked Christ to come into your heart, ask the Holy Spirit to flood your soul with Divine power. It is impossible to be in the center of God's will continually without knowing the guidance of the Holy Spirit. He is the Master Guide and the "dynamite" of God's power.

(2) *Be sure you have fully YIELDED yourself to the will of God.* It's not what YOU want, it's what *HE* wants! God can't direct a life that doesn't *want* to be directed. You must ask Him to totally direct your will. Now, is this unreasonable? He knows what the future holds — you don't. And who is best equipped to run your life — you or God? He has all wisdom and power, and the ability to be with you wherever you go. Nothing is too hard for Him. He has never made a mistake, never had to say, "I don't know." And He has never made a selfish decision. You don't have to be afraid of surrender to Him. He is a loving, kind, and compassionate Father Who longs for your highest happiness and holiness. Make it a matter of sincere and heart-felt prayer and self-searching. Then tell Him you are willing to go *wherever* He wants you to go, and do *whatever* He wants you to do — no matter what the cost. If you don't *mean* it — don't pray. God will take you up on any promise you make to Him.

(3) *Count the cost.* A half-hearted "Christianity" is power-less and joyless. ALL—or NOTHING—is God's standard of committal. God never uses people whom He can get rid of easily. He never does busi-ness with people who don't mean business with Him. Now — are you willing? Think SPECIFICALLY. Are you ready to *leave home*? Give up your *rights* to a home? *Friends? Family? Marriage?* A specially-lucrative or impor-tant *career* you have followed since you were little? Re-member the story of Abra-ham. God may not ask you to give up or sacrifice your rights

to *any* of these — but unless you are WILLING — honestly willing to do so, forget about Him ever using you. This is going to be hard — really hard. But if you really mean business with God — and you do — you won't want it any other way. The BEST things cost the MOST.

(4) *Ask Him to SHOW you.* Don't expect that God will always DETAIL everything for you, or tell you in advance all that He has in store for you. As men's choices change, so God changes the ways that *He* works. Don't get mad at God because He doesn't show you a diary of the next five years of your life. Such a diary is impossible because you are a moral creature.

Every choice you make brings into being *brand-new creations* in God's universe. God will use these to fulfill His own purposes. But because they don't exist until you actually *make* them, it is impossible to give you a detailed "diary" of your life in future. You will not find the word "plan" or "blueprint" in the Scriptures. You have been made free to choose, and for this reason, it is important that you learn to know God's voice on a DAY-TO-DAY basis. You can expect guidance for what you have to do RIGHT AWAY: but He may not always show you what you are supposed to do next *year!* And don't be hung up on words or definitions of your ministry for Him — God may call you to do something, then change it later as He feels you are better equipped to handle another task. The only thing you can be sure of is that He *will use* you wherever He wants you and that you can expect Him to show you what to do in each circumstance.

Don't be too impatient. A walk with God is *one step at a time*. He will never forget you. He will never be late in His promises. FAILURE can only come from your side. But there never need be disappointment, or the sense of having missed His will — if you WANT to know Him — if you WANT to know your task for the present with all your heart.

RECOGNIZING GUIDANCE

How will God speak to you?

God has guided people in history, and in the Bible in many ways. Sometimes these were *supernatural* ways, like the burning bush that Moses saw, or the Voice that little Samuel heard; or the light that blinded the young zealous Pharisee who later became the apostle Paul. In revivals of faith down through the centuries, there have been recurring instances of guidance like this. He has done it before with His men and women, and He may also guide you in the same way today. But on the daily pathway of life, you can expect that more special form of guidance that Elijah knew — the "still, small voice."

Knowing God by direct, quiet, and loving communion honors His love more than always needing to have great displays of supernatural direction. Think of a Father in a home of great wealth and power. Which do you think would honor him more when he wants his boys and girls to listen to what he says — putting on a "sky-writing team" to lay out his instructions for the day, writing them in neon lights, or even having to speak to them in person before they will do what they *know* He wants done —

or the pleasure of just watching them read the books He has left in the house about His aims and duties and doing what He wants out of love for Who He is and knowing what He has His *heart* set on? Sometimes God must use "supernatural" means to get through to us, but often this is because we are too hard of hearing spiritually to know what He wants in any other way. God never shows off. He is humble, in all His greatness. But you *can* expect Him to speak to you, whether it is by one of the strange and supernatural ways of the Bible, or the still small voice.

THE THREE C's OF GUIDANCE

(1) *CONVICTION:* A deep-down sense of the right thing to do that comes from the guidance of the Holy Spirit and a

clear conscience. From reading God's Word, from prayer, and working for the Lord from day to day, God will surely and steadily make clear what He wants you to do. *Never act out of doubt*. If you are unsure that this is the right step, don't move until you feel clear before God. The Bible says "Whatsoever is not of faith is sin." If you cannot go ahead with a clear heart and a free spirit, don't move. If you find that while in prayer or in daily work for the Lord, something keeps on coming back to you (not like a "flash" or in a sudden, dramatic burst in your mind, but just a steady, returning "nudge" in your mind and spirit). Listen. God often keeps bringing things to our mind that He wants us to act on. If you get really excited about something everytime you are close to God and you *hear* about that "something," listen again. It may be God speaking to you. Conviction is something that "grows" on you. If it is of God, you will *never* shake it off. And if a conviction is rejected, there will be a deep sense of loss and a knowledge that you have missed the voice of God in that situation.

The Lord Jesus said, "My sheep *hear* My voice, and I know them, and they follow Me." (John 10:27) If we belong to the fold of God, we have Jesus' promise that we will know His voice.

(2) *CIRCUMSTANCE:* God will often close or open doors to help you see what His will is. You may set out to do something and find out that everything falls apart; it doesn't hang together, or go right, even when you pray about it. This may be God blocking a wrong path when you have missed His directions. On the other hand, after you feel something in your heart that you believe might be God's direction, an opportunity may occur in the most unexpected place. If you are trying to follow God's will as honestly as you know how, don't be afraid that you will make an irreparable mistake. Sometimes it will be a little hard to determine exactly what God is saying to you; and many times, doing what He seems to be saying involves a risk to your reputation, your pride, or your popularity. But if we really love God, and walk in the light of His word, He will go before us to prepare the way. "Circumstance" guidance is like walking up to the door of a big supermarket or

department store with automatic doors; you walk up to the door, and just as you think you are going to hit the glass, the door swings aside and you go through. Push forwards, and let God swing open the doors of circumstance as a help in confirmation of His will.

(3) *CONFIRMATION:* God may find other ways to confirm to you what He wants done. Sometimes this may come in the form of a *dream* or a *sign* of some kind. Gideon used a "fleece" before the Lord because he was afraid and unsure of His voice. Don't go around "fleecing" the Lord all the time, even though He will honor the "fleeces" young Christians put out sometimes to encourage their faith in Him. But learn to expect *some* form of confirmation, especially from the *Bible*. The greater the decision you have to make, the greater the right you have to expect that the Lord will make His will abundantly clear to you. Ask God for scriptures to deny or confirm what you feel in your heart and what circumstances seem to be leading you towards. But if He confirms something clearly — DO IT! If you dishonor Him by repeatedly asking for more "signs" when His will is plain, He will take from you the assurance you already have; and you will be left in a confusion which only sincere repentance will deliver you from.

By the way, don't expect Him to tell you in the *same* way He told someone else. He delights in using different ways to guide His children. Let it be a special surprise to you; don't tell Him how you want Him to guide you. Just wait His time.

NO MOANS

While God makes plain His will for you, there are some things you can do in the meanwhile, in the years when you are seeking to know His purpose for your life. Don't be worried if you don't immediately know the night after you give your life to Jesus what God wants you to do! Sometimes He puts us through *training* to see if He can trust us before He will make clear what He has on His heart for us. Use the years of your early conversion to learn discipline and obedience from Him, and expect that He will open up the pathway for you.

In the meantime —

(1) *Follow your INTERESTS and ABILITIES*. Find out what you can do well, and what you can't. Sometimes our backgrounds are part of God's purpose for us; the lessons we have learned from life, the responses and the choices we have made in the past are all used by the Lord and woven into His ultimate purposes. God wants to use us — *as we are*. You are different from anyone else in the world. Find out what makes you *special*. Sometimes God may use your talents; sometimes it is your very lack of talents that make you very special to Him. Hudson Taylor said, "When God wanted to evangelize China, He looked for a man *WEAK ENOUGH* to use." Learn what you like to do well and what abilities you have.

(2) *HAVE MANY INTERESTS* in your teenage years. Learn to do a lot of things, and be interested in more than just a few things you have already done. Try your hand out in different *sports*; they may help develop your body in different ways that will make it stronger and more serviceable for Jesus in the years ahead. Experiment with different hobbies — some of the things you learn in recreation times will become valuable tools in the future; especially ones like radio or electronics, photography, art or crafts. Try to DEVELOP the capabilities God has entrusted to you. Be ENTHUSIASTIC about what you do! Really get into it, and get an interest in as many things as you can. The more things you know a little about, the more people you may be able to reach for Jesus.

(3) *READ ABOUT the things you'd like to do*. If you think God might be calling you to some form of *missionary* work,

read biographies of famous missionaries. If you think God has called you to be a Christian artist, or a mechanic, or a scientist, read books about art, mechanics, and science. Read often and wisely. If you learn to like books, you'll have a wider picture of the world God wants to reach.

(4) *Get some PRACTICAL EXPERIENCE early.* Take *a part-time job* in the area of your interest. During holidays or vacation times, ask if you can just do some odd job around the place you would like to work in, and talk to others already on that job. On spare time, ask a lot of questions. Do they find it interesting? What does it cost in terms of time, study, and commitment? Can you advance in it? Will it take care of your financial needs? Of course, all jobs must be those that will honor God and help forward His creation; anything that is shady or morally tainted is totally off-limits to the child of God.

(5) *STUDY God's word.* Even secular jobs will benefit from a year or so in a good part time Bible school or correspondence course in Scripture. And PRAY; talk over new developments and disappointments with Jesus.

A CHALLENGE

Whether you like it or not, you are now in the most decisive years of the world's history. *Never before* has there been a more strategic hour . . . Never before has dedication to the Lord Jesus Christ been more important than it is for you today! Longfellow, prophetically it seems, wrote: "Humanity with all its fears — with all its hopes for future years — is hanging, breathless on THY fate."

You may be the most important young person in the world — because in a few year's time, as world population hits an explosive FOUR BILLION, YOU may be the man or woman to whom the Christian world will look for leadership or inspiration to postpone God's final judgement, and bring in one last great revival of righteousness to our generation!

A sixteen-year-old named Valadmir Ulynov saw soldiers hang his brother for treason, and made up his mind to CHANGE THE WORLD. Because of that decision, nearly half the world is in slavery today! As he stood there in hurt and anger and grief, he bitterly said, "I'll make them pay for it. I swear I'll make them pay!" A contemptuous adult beside him said with a sneer, "You'll make who pay?" the boy said, "*Never mind. I know.*" A few years later, that young man changed his name. They called him LENIN, man of steel. A compatriot said to a friend on seeing this young, committed man, "I am afraid of that young man." His friend asked, "Why are you afraid?" He said, "Because he is the only man I know *who thinks and dreams of nothing but revolution twenty-four hours a day*." And that young man made the world pay for his brother's death. Under his discipline and genius, the ideas of Karl Marx and Engels were forged into a military, militant machine that changed the face of the world in less than sixty years in the *communist revolution*.

Now is the time for God to find the holy rebels, the radicals for righteousness. YOUR degree of dedication, YOUR willingness to sacrifice for God's glory, your availability for service — these are the weapons which alone will decide whether our generation will be marked by the sign of the fish or the slash of the sword; whether we will name the age for Christ or see it named for Satan. This is the generation of the *Jesus revolution*, and what we do with the world God has thrust into our hands will decide its future. In our time, there are nearly more people living than there have *ever* been in all of the years of man up to this present time, and what we do with His commission and His enabling may help decide whether heaven will have a larger population than hell.

But only the DEDICATED will win. "True Christianity is an all-out commitment to Jesus Christ. God has called us to WORLD DOMINION. A critical world is watching. By some strange instinct, it realizes that the Christian life deserves EVERYTHING — or NOTHING." Count the COST of the way of the cross! (Luke 14: 25-33) God can use you — God WILL use you; if you are willing to pay the price, the high cost of Christ — absolute obedience to His will!

DOORWAYS TO DISCIPLESHIP TEST

INSTRUCTIONS:

1. FIRST, ANSWER THE FOUR SETS OF QUESTIONS IN THE FOLLOWING TWO PAGES OF THIS TEST. MARK THE HONEST ANSWER YOU CAN GIVE TO EACH WITH A "YES" OR A "NO."

2. NEXT, USING YOUR QUESTION SHEET, WITH YOUR MARKED ANSWERS, SHADE IN ALL AREAS YOU COULD HONESTLY MARK "YES." (YOU MAY LIKE TO USE DIFFERENT COLORS FOR EACH AREA.)

This revolution begins in a home — the home of your life, which you have hopefully given to God for His service. There may well be *doors* of that house that the Lord Jesus has never been given access to. This searching little test will help you find out just how far *your* dedication to Jesus really has gone. Each section of the following chart represents a "doorway" to Christian discipleship in the home of your very own being. You will be asked some straight questions about each "door." Go through these questions *prayerfully* and *carefully* before God. Answer them as *honestly* as you can. This test is between you and God alone. If you cannot say a definite, positive "yes", then mark your answer *"NO"*. You may *shade in* every area where you have a "YES" answer; leave BLANK those you had to say "NO" to.

Ready? All you need is a *pencil*, a word of *prayer* — and total honesty before God.

MENTAL — "Let this mind be in you which was also in Christ Jesus." (Philippians 2:5)

(1) *BASEMENT* (Motives) — The foundation of your whole life. God does not ask "What?" as much as He asks "Why?" Here are the first two, most searching questions of your life — *WHY* are *you* doing what you are doing, and *WHO* are *you* REALLY LIVING FOR? No matter what you do, or who you are, the *real* test of whether you are a true child of God lies here at the "basement" door. Have you given this first room, this most important room, to the Lord? Have you stopped living for yourself, and begun to live for Jesus?

☐ *Yes* ☐ *No* — I have honestly made a choice to give myself wholly to Christ.

(2) *GALLERY* (Meditation) — Your attitudes formed by what you think about are like a picture gallery in your mind. It is important to take time to meditate on the important things, for this will help you understand, evaluate, and apply what you learn. It prevents hasty decision and tragic false moves; it teaches you to WAIT on the Lord. How is your reflection time?

☐ *Yes* ☐ *No* — I have a place in my daily life for thinking things over with God.

(3) *STUDY* (Training) — A vitally important area is your *academic* life. The success or the failure of you effectively

reaching a teacher, official, worker, or classmate often depends on your scholastic effort. For a Christian, it is classroom *and* witness suicide to "forget to do" assignments, "cop-out" of class, or fail a test or examination through laziness or sheer carelessness. This doesn't mean you have to be a genius at everything, but it *does* mean that you must "study to show yourself approved to God" and do the very best you can.

☐ *Yes*   ☐ *No* — I can honestly say I have given my study life to God for His glory.

(4) *LIBRARY (Thoughts)* — Your thought-life feeds your attitudes, and these in turn shape your actions. What books of thought you place on the "library shelves" of your mind will, to a large extent, determine what kind of person you are, and will be. If your library is simply a garbage collection of trash, obscenity, and filth, your thought-life will be the same. Don't get me wrong — everyone has an occasional wrong thought, which can be resisted. I'm talking about the mind that is continually in the gutter. How is YOUR thought-life, friend?

☐ *Yes*   ☐ *No* — My thought life is controlled by the Mind of the Master, Jesus.

PHYSICAL — "What? Know you not that your body is the temple of the Holy Spirit which is in you, which you have of God, and you are not your own? For you are bought with a price: therefore glorify God in your body, and in your spirit, which are God's." (I Corinthians 6:19-20)

Our earthly bodies have been given to us for a short time here on earth, and God expects us to take proper care of them for Him. He must have full control of your physical life.

(5) *DRESSING ROOM (Appearance)* — "First impressions are most important." Good grooming is essential to your witness; the way you dress, the condition of your clothes,

whether you wear the right kind of things at the right time — all may help or hinder your outreach to others. It is quite impossible to dress without being drab or "out", and not draw too much attention to yourself.

☐ *Yes* ☐ *No* — My personal appearance contributes positively to my witness.

(6) *WORKSHOP (Abilities)* —What God has given you in the way of talents, gifts, and capability. Everybody has at least ONE talent — even if it's only to smile! It's fun to discover and develop your abilities, but you must be sure they have all been given wholly to God to use.

☐ *Yes* ☐ *No* — Each talent, ability, or gift I have has been fully surrendered to God for Him to use, even if He should want me to *give it up* for Him and do something else.

(7) *BATHROOM (Cleanliness)* — Care of your body is vital. You can be a groovy guy or girl, but it won't mean much if you fail to take care of the little things — like care of your hair, nails, teeth, and skin. Toothpaste, soap, and deodorant have a purpose — can you guess it?

☐ *Yes* ☐ *No* — Since I care for it properly, my body does not hinder my outreach.

(8) *COURTYARD (Control)* — You are developing new drives, and one of the biggest problems you will face is the one in the courtyard — dating and the channeling of the sex drive. These years can be exciting and wonderful, but you may get badly burned if you abuse your body and indulge in relationships that violate the commands of Christ. God cannot use you if you are in a parked car necking, petting up a storm, or having a field day at someone else's expense. Are your drives in Christ's control? Honestly now — how about your date life?

☐ *Yes* ☐ *No* — My drives and date life are under the control and discipline of God.

SPIRITUAL — "Grow in grace and in the knowledge of our Lord and Saviour Jesus Christ . . . and to know the love of Christ, which passes knowledge, that you might be filled with all the fullness of God." (II Peter 3:18 and Ephesians 3:19 combined.)

The spiritual central rooms of your life are the inner centers of *all* other areas of your being, and determine the extent and strength of your vitality in Christ. Surrendering the keys to these doors will be essential for you to live, love, and enjoy being a child of God.

(9) *KITCHEN (Word of God)* — Do you spend even *half* as much time in the *spiritual* kitchen of your life as you do in your outside life? A great deal of problems you face could be simply answered by the Word of God — IF you read it *often* enough! "A chapter a day keeps the devil away" someone said, but it may take a lot more than a hurried skim last thing at night or a few seconds before breakfast to give you the answers you need.

☐ *Yes*   ☐ *No* — I have a daily appointment with the Word of God to learn, read, and study it so I might be equipped to deal with difficulties in my life and others I meet.

(10) *DRAWING ROOM (Witness)* — Sharing your faith in Christ with others. This is the only real reason why God keeps us here — apart from the lessons we can learn when we become His children — to *share* what the Lord Jesus can do to others who do not know Him. It is our greatest earthly responsibility and one of our highest privileges — representing Him.

☐ *Yes*   ☐ *No* — My other surrendered "rooms," Bible-study, and prayer-times all work together to help me tell others of Jesus whenever the opportunity arises; and I can tell others what God has done for me in a way that God will honor to bring results for Him.

(11) *CLOSET (Prayer)* — A daily time set aside to talk over problems with the Lord and share blessings with Him — to tell Him how much you love Him, to be honest with Him about your problems and doubts, and to learn to listen to His still, small Voice. No work for God ever gets off the ground or brings lasting results without this all-important factor behind it.

☐ *Yes*   ☐ *No* — I have a daily prayer-life that gets results and answers from God, and I don't forget to spend time in thanking Him for Who He is and What He has done.

(12) *GENERATOR ROOM (Power)* — The hidden room that is the source of energy to the whole house is the cell of *obedience* to God. To the Lord Jesus Christ, nothing matters like a whole-hearted obedience to DO what He asks us to without complaint. The Holy Spirit will not only direct and empower our lives if we are willing to do WHATEVER God asks us.

☐ *Yes*   ☐ *No* — I have made a *conscious surrender* to the will of God, and asked Him for the power of His Holy Spirit to direct, purify, and empower my life for His glory.

SOCIAL — "Whatever you do in word or deed, do everything in the Name of the Lord Jesus, and through Him give thanks to the Father." (Colossians 3:17)

When the personal rooms of your life have been wholly given to the Lord Jesus the other four rooms that involve your relationships with others must also be turned over to Him. Tragedy strikes here all too often, in the areas of friendships, family, and activities.

(13) *GUESTROOM (Friends)* — Either *you* will control your friendships or your friendships will control YOU! What *kind* of friends you most like to be with is a very revealing sign of what kind of person YOU are really like inside. Every Christian must be a friend of sinners, like

Jesus was when He walked the earth; but our *closest* circle of friendships must be with those of the family of God. This especially included girl and boyfriends!

☐ *Yes* ☐ *No* — My friendships are all made in the Lord, no single friend of mine comes practically before Christ in my affections, and my friendships made with those who do not yet know the Lord are the result of a primary motive to bring them to Jesus.

(14) *LIVING ROOM (Family)* There is no greater test of your Christian life than in the home. It is in the *family* that God will test your willingness to follow Him without complaint, and to submit to the discipline of correction and reproof. Whatever problems your own home or family life has had, have you made a conscious effort to *do* what God has asked you to do in your home for His sake? Have you been willing to forgive, to love your parents?

☐ *Yes* ☐ *No* — I have put my whole family situation in the hands of the Lord Jesus.

(15) *OFFICE (Authority)* —Most young people have some measure of result-getting leadership ability in one or more fields of interest — the sciences, arts, humanities, or sports fields. One of the most powerful avenues of Christian witness you can develop is to give Christ the key to your office room of authority. He will be able to help you *develop* your leadership ability, and place you in vital positions of responsibility where you can work for Him.

☐ *Yes* ☐ *No* — I have given my leadership ability and authority to the Lord, with all rights to my life, and am now developing this to create new chances to witness for God.

(16) *RUMPUS ROOM (Activities)* — Billy Graham once said, "You tell me what you do with your spare time, and I'll tell you what kind of young person you are." One of the greatest sins of youth today is the sin of *wasting God's time.*

The Bible outlines clear spiritual principles by which you can judge your activities and form convictions as to which is right and which is wrong. All things are to be done "as unto the Lord," including the way you behave at home, at school, and at outings or vacations. Is *God* in charge of your rumpus-room?

☐ *Yes* ☐ *No* — I plan and carry out my activities with the glory of God as my final purpose, and am able to bring the Lord Jesus with me in all my work and pleasure times.

DOORWAYS TO DISCIPLESHIP

MENTAL　　　　　　　　　　　　　　　　**PHYSICAL**
Phillipians 2:5　　　　　　　　　I Corinthians 6:19-20

BASEMENT (Motives) Proverbs 4:23	GALLERY (Meditation) Phillipians 4:8	DRESSING ROOM (Appearance) I Thessalonians 5:22	WORKSHOP (Abilities) Colossians 3:23
STUDY (Training) IITimothy 2:15	LIBRARY (Thoughts) Proverbs 23:7	BATHROOM (Cleanliness) Hebrews 10:22	COURTYARD (Control) I Thessalonians 4:4

KITCHEN (Word of God) Matthew 5:6	DRAWING ROOM (Witness) John 12:32	GUEST ROOM (Friends) Amos 3:3	LIVING ROOM (Family) Romans 12:18
CLOSET (Prayer) Matthew 6:6	GENERATOR (Power) Acts 1:8	OFFICE (Authority) Psalms 75:6-7	RUMPUS ROOM (Activities) Colossians 3:17

SPIRITUAL　　　　　　　　　　　　　　　**SOCIAL**
II Peter 3:18;　　　　　　　　Colossians 3:17
Ephesians 3:19

SHADE IN each area when you have made a full committal of it to the Lord Jesus. This chart will serve as a blueprint of your own spiritual, mental, physical, and social development with God and others. *Y*ou will become a world-changer when Christ has *all* the keys! Begin to work on those unshaded areas at once. Your move!

HOW TO BE SAVED!

GOD LOVES YOU!

He **made** you. He knows how you feel. He understands **all** your problems. He knows your background. He knows your name. And God **loves** you and wants you to have the best for your life.

Everything God does, He does out of **love**. His love is not just a good feeling about His Universe, but an unselfish CHOICE to **will our highest good.**

"Herein is love; not that **we** loved God, but that He loves **us** and sent His Son to be the way through which we could be forgiven and come back to Him."

SIN has come between you and God. Sin is really **selfishness;** a "me first" attitude of heart and life. It is denying God's right to be God in your life; it is breaking His laws, and scorning His guidelines for happiness.

It is **putting ourselves first** above everyone else; living first of all to serve and please ME instead of God, and refusing to treat all others according to their rightful place and value in the Universe.

"And **this** is the condemnation, that light is come into the world; and men loved darkness rather than light, because their deeds were evil . . ." "ALL have sinned and come short of the glory of God."

GOD HATES SIN because it costs so much. Sin is the cause of all the heartache in our world. God didn't plan sin. He never plans unhappiness. He wants man to be happy and free. Sin is the reason why there is pain, misery and death in our land. Sin enslaves us to our feelings instead of doing what is right and reasonable. Sin makes us feel guilty, afraid and alone. **Sin is the most expensive thing in the Universe.** It cost **God** His only Son; it cost Jesus Christ His **life.** God, Who must be just, **never** can allow sin to go unpunished, or the Universe would begin to collapse in evil. When God's infinitely important law of love for happiness is broken, the law-breaker **must** pay the penalty. A law without a penalty is only **advice.** The penalty must be important as the law it is designed to protect. For such a terribly **important** law as God's law, which was made to direct and protect His intelligent, moral creatures, God set a penalty as high as possible — **endless** death, or separation forever from His Universe and all the rights and privileges of living and growing in it through eternity. "The soul that sins **shall** die . . . The wages of sin is death."

YOU, as a sinner, deserve to be punished. You know that deep inside. By rights, you should pay the penalty of your sin. You **knew** what was right, but did not do it. You have made a mess of your life. If you are really **honest**, you know you have no excuses to make. **Nothing** you could say to God could possibly justify the choices you have made to please yourself.

"Knowing that a man is not justified by the works of law . . . for by the works of the law shall no flesh be justified . . . If we say we have not sinned, we make Him a liar and His Word is not in us."

BUT — IN HIS GREAT LOVE AND WISDOM, **GOD FOUND A WAY TO FORGIVE YOU, AND STILL** BE **JUST IF** . . . . YOU ARE WILLING TO MEET HIS **CONDITIONS. . . .**

The Lord Jeseus humbled Himself and became man. He lived a perfect life and never broke His Father's law of love. He offered His own perfect life as a sacrifice to provide a substitute for the penalty of **your** sin. His death on the cross shows at once how much God loves you and how much He hates your sin. You can choose one of two things; pay the penalty for your sin, OR resolve to turn your back on the past and give your life to God, letting the Lord Jesus be your substitute. God CANNOT forgive you **unless** you are willing to stop fighting Him and make Him your Boss. His Holy Spriit makes you willing to change, as He draws you now by His love. He wants to help you make a life-changing decision NOW. **Jesus** said -

"I am the Way, the Truth and the Life; no man comes to the Father but by Me . He that trusts his life wholly to the Son is experiencing eternal life; he that does not believe on on the Son of God shall not see life; but the anger of God abides on him."

SALVATION is God's plan to restore man to a holy, happy relationship with Him. All problems of sin, doubt, failure, lack of victory or insufficiency of God's power can be conquered by the following steps:

1. **RETHINK** - - - Stop running away from the Voice of God and look at your life. We do not naturally **want** to obey God; only if we let the Holy Spirit show us our sin as GOD sees it will we realize just how bad we have been. To do this, you MUST be TOTALLY HONEST!
Don't **pretend**.
Don't play down your sin.
Stop making **excuses!**
Admit it from your **heart**; "God, I am all wrong"!
If necessary, get paper and pencil and WRITE DOWN the things that have come between you and God, and stopped you from serving Him as you ought to.

2. **REPENT** - - - Turn your back on your old way of life. Be WILLING to **lose** any habit, any plan, any friend that you have been living your life for instead of God. This is not easy, but Jesus said if we wanted to follow Him, we must first **count the cost. (Luke 14:25-33)** Salvation is like a real marriage. Two people promise themselves to each other, pledge their love to each other before a watching world, and give up all their old dates. This is what God wants you to do to know His love.

3. **RENOUNCE** - - - Give up all **RIGHTS** to your own life. If you are going to be a part of God's world-changing family, you cannot be your **own** boss any longer. You must **DIE** to your own plans, dreams and ambitions and be willing to do whatever God wants you to do. He knows EXACTLY what will make you most happy. It may hurt to surrender everything at first, but God knows best, and will **never** ask you to do anything that you will regret in the end. A true Christian has nothing of his own; time, talents, money, possessions, friends, career and future - - all must be surrendered for his King's service wherever and whenever He wants them.

4. REPLAN --- Be prepared to make many **changes** in your life! The very moment you make this heart-choice for God, the old you will die, and a new person inside you will begin to live. If the Holy Spirit is speaking to you about getting something with someone, you must be **willing** to do it in order for God to help you. Wherever you need to confess wrong, or restore or repay something to someone, the Lord Jesus will give you the courage and the words to say. Becoming a Christian implies the WILLINGNESS, as far as humanly possible, to **right all known wrong.** (Prov. 28:13)

If you have written out a list of things that have come between you and God, as NOW His forgiveness for those against Him; plan to make right all others with people you know you have wronged, and feel guilty about. The circle of **confession** must fit the circle of committal of sin. Those against **God**, confess **only to HIM**; those against one person, to **that** person alone; those against a **group**, to the **group**.

5. RECEIVE – You must take the Lord Jesus Christ by FAITH (a loyalty of love to the Word of God) to **rule in your heart as King.** He must be your absolute **"Boss"** from now on! This act of faith is neither an "idea" or a mere "feeling" but an ACT, a CHOICE of your WILL, made **intelligently and carefully.** Give Him your doubts, your weakness and your loneliness. Your heart will never have peace, your doubts will never clear up, you will never die to the world until you trust, surrender, BELIEVE from your heart! **Be totally honest with Him.** Receive Christ into your life as your Lord and Master, to live for Him from this moment on, forever. (Rom. 10: 9-10)

THERE IS NO TIME LIKE **NOW** ...
READY? ... GOD HAS DONE **ALL HE CAN** FOR
YOU ...
THE NEXT MOVE MUST BE **YOURS**!!!!

Are you willing to trust His love? Will you choose His life, or turn your back on His love and choose a future without Christ, without hope and without an end? **Will you be very honest with Him right now?** Talk to God before the touch of His Holy Spirit lifts off your life. **Tell Him in your own words** something like this:

> *"God, I'm sorry I've been selfish and rebellious so long. I'm sick of my old life and I want to change. Please forgive my sin, and give me the power to live my life from this moment on for You. I give You my heart; take over everything I have and am, and be my Lord and King. Amen."*

WELCOME to the family!

If you have surrendered your life to the Lordship of Jesus Christ, you have entered an exciting new world. Things should be different, life will be fresh and new. If God has really taken the throne of your heart, you will start noticing many "new" things happening in your life. Please continue reading this book to learn how to **live** your Christian life.

SYMPTOM INDEX

This index will enable you to use *Doorways To Discipleship* as a *spiritual check-up*. Find your particular problem here; beside it are the pages that will best cover the spiritual remedy you need

**Read The Books By Other Communications Founda-
tion Authors:** Mrs. Gwen Wilkerson (Wife Of David Wilkerson—Author Of "The Cross & The Switchblade); Har-
old Brinkley, Tony Salerno, Sr., And Bob Maddox.

**Hear The Cassette Tapes Of Communication Founda-
tion Speakers Such As:** A. W. Tozer, Juan Carlos Ortiz,
Winkie Pratney, And Tony Salerno, Jr.

COMMUNICATION FOUNDATION
Box 386
Lindale, Texas 75771
(214) 882-5571

RUSH YOUR ORDER IN TODAY!

QTY.	BOOKS BY WINKIE PRATNEY	TOTAL
_____	Christian Growth Series (14 booklets) @$6.50	_____
	CASSETTE TAPES BY WINKIE PRATNEY	
_____	How To Be Religious Without Being a Christian ...@$3.95	_____
_____	Witnessing Like Jesus @$3.95	_____
_____	Change Your Conduct Or Change Your Name @$3.95	_____
_____	Free Catalog of other C. F. Growth Products	FREE
	SUB TOTAL	_____

FREE SHIPPING ON ORDERS
OVER $5.00 (30¢ if less)

TOTAL ENCLOSED
WITH ORDER _____

PLEASE RUSH THIS ORDER TO:

NAME _____
      FIRST   LAST

ADDRESS _____
         STREET

_____
    CITY   STATE   ZIP

For a free catalog containing other books
and literature by Winkie Pratney
plus other Christian growth materials
and tapes, please write;

COMMUNICATION FOUNDATION
P. O. BOX 386
LINDALE, TEXAS 75771

Communication Foundation is a ministry of
AGAPE FORCE